D1554523

TIME MANAGEMENT FOR TEENS AND COLLEGE STUDENTS

THE ULTIMATE GUIDE FOR BALANCING
SCHOOL AND LIFE FOR TEENS AND YOUNG
ADULTS

KARA ROSS

PUBLISHING FORTE

INTRODUCTION

Being good at managing your time can be beneficial, and it doesn't matter if you are a parent, student, just working a job, or managing a small business. When it comes to our daily lives, we all have 24 hours or less to get all we need done, and many times the thought of so little time and so much to do can be very overwhelming. Many of us strive to do as much as we can as best we can before this time runs out. It sometimes feels like no matter how hard we try, we just can never catch up. It frightens us too because we often realize that if we don't manage our time well enough to get certain things done, it can have severe repercussions on our lives regarding family, friends, school, and work.

We sometimes don't have time to do what's good for our bodies, spend time with our family and friends, or get everything done at work. In the long run, when we fail at these parts of our lives, we feel dissatisfied and as though life is a fast-track hustle, just enough time to do the bare minimum. Sounds familiar, right? But what if I told you that there is a way to do all that you need and want to, a way to make your days a lot more fulfilling and effective?. I will show you ways to manage your time better and get more of what you want out of every day in just a few simple steps.

I will show you what you can do to get the most out of your time. I will reveal things that you may never notice and some that you never really thought were linked to helping you better manage and take control of your time. All that I have written has been tested and proven through my experiences. That being said, feel free to take what helps you and also feel free to leave behind what doesn't.

Let's get started, shall we?

1

GOAL SETTING MADE SIMPLE

To acquire what you want out of life, you must first understand what you desire. After all, how can you reach your full potential if you have no idea where you want to go, who you are, or what brings you joy?

MOST OF YOU are undoubtedly thinking to yourselves, "I have no idea what I want to accomplish with my life!" That is perfectly acceptable and expected. It takes time to figure out life's big questions, and goal setting is such an important part of that process. Learning how to use objectives effectively to get the most out of your life is an important skill to master. If you don't know what you want to achieve in life, it's like embarking on a journey with no clear endpoint. Even if you enjoy the ride, you're still going to risk winding up somewhere you don't want to be, and you're not going to choose the most efficient way!

ISN'T IT STRAIGHTFORWARD? You must first ask yourself what you truly desire in life and then go out and acquire it. Right?

. . .

UNFORTUNATELY, this is not the case. Goal formulation is far from simple and requires much skill. The difficulty is that few individuals are aware of this, never considering evaluating the goals themselves. They place the blame on their motivation, circumstances, or even other individuals. However, they rarely think about whether the problem is with their own objectives.

WHAT ARE YOUR OBJECTIVES? What exactly are your objectives? Do you want to make the Dean's List, find your calling, get a job, or ~~get by with a mediocre degree~~? Everyone needs goals, and identifying them ahead of time will help you stay focused along the road.

WHAT ARE the benefits of setting goals? Life is chaotic and tends to slip away from you. There are thousands of possibilities at any given time, including new bright, flashy products, a new viral cat video, a few hundred social media updates from friends, and a slew of other activities. You took driver's education, practiced for hours on end, and learned the rules of the road as you prepared to receive your driver's license. You didn't just get in the car and decide to drive to Alaska to see some Kodiak bears and demonstrate your wonderful driving skills along the way when you went for your driver's exam, and the tester told you where to go, where to turn left, right, speed up, turn around, and so on. But what's keeping you from settling in Alaska? The explanation is that you got into your automobile with a specific aim in mind: to obtain the driver's license you'd wished for/years! You knew exactly what you wanted to do from the start, and you had a clear plan that you stuck to.

. . .

IT's the same way in life. If you know where you want to go from the start, you'll most likely get there. You'll get there eventually, even if there are some delays. However, if you don't know where you're heading, you're unlikely to arrive at a pleasant place.   ← *not true*

An Example of Bad Goal Setting

To understand how to write a good goal, it can help first to look at what makes a bad goal. Why is it that some goals don't work out the way they should? What should we do differently to avoid this happening the next time?

LET's imagine for a moment that you want to get into shape. You're planning on losing weight and building muscle – which is a pretty common goal that an awful lot of people are interested in accomplishing.

IN THIS EXAMPLE, a typical goal might involve writing down the ideal body weight and measurements you are trying to reach and then setting yourself a target – three months, six months, or one year. And then you get to it! But, this is a goal that is destined to fail. Why? Because this goal is far too vague, far too distant, and far too out of your control.

LET's fast forward two weeks, at which point you have hopefully been training hard for a while and changing your diet. Suddenly, life starts to get in the way. You find yourself bogged down with other things you have to do like that upcoming exam, paper, or party on Friday night, and you don't have the time or energy to make it to the gym today. Or tomorrow. And the day after that is looking shaky as well.

BUT YOU TELL yourself it is okay because you don't need to work out. Not working out on those days is not breaking your goal. You have plenty of time to reach your goal, and it is up to you how you will go about making it happen. So, if you take time off today, you'll just put some more time in tomorrow. Or the next day. If this week is a write-off, then you can always make up for it next week.

AND SO, it continues, week after week, until you get to the end of your allotted period and you realize you've blown any chance of accomplishing that goal.

OR HOW ABOUT this alternative scenario? Imagine that you put in the time and worked very hard every day to get into shape. But the pounds just didn't come off. Maybe this is due to slow metabolism; perhaps it boils down to those late-night snacks or just too much partying.

EITHER WAY, you get to a certain point, and you realize once again that you aren't going to make it even though you tried your best. So, what do you do? You give up, disheartened, and you quit trying.

A Better Goal

Now let's imagine that same scenario, but this time, we approach our goal differently. What would a good goal look like if you wanted to lose weight or build muscle?

FOR STARTERS, you should remove the time element. Instead of aiming to accomplish something in X number of days, how about you aim to do something toward your goal every day. Look at the goal that you want to accomplish and then break that down into much smaller steps. To lose weight, let's say you need to eat 1,800 calories or less a day. And you need to work out three times a week for an hour each day. If you can stick to this plan, you will eventually notice changes – be they big or small.

INSTEAD OF FOCUSING on the end goal, set yourself a daily plan. A daily goal is something that is entirely within your control – meaning that you cannot "fail" for reasons outside of your control. It is also completely resistant to being put off or delayed. You can't "work out today" tomorrow! Likewise, slow metabolism isn't going to prevent you from eating only 1,800 calories.

I LEARNED this concept from actor/comedian Jerry Seinfeld. Jerry developed a technique that he uses to make sure he sticks to these kinds of goals, and he calls it "The Chain." The idea is that he builds a chain each day as he completes his daily goal, each day represents a new link in his chain, and this process creates immense pressure not to break the chain. For Jerry, the process of writing one new joke each day allowed him to craft his skills and provided the foundation for his tremendous long-term success.

An easy way to implement this strategy is with a calendar and a pen. Every day that you successfully achieve 1,800 calories or less, you put a tick on the calendar for that day. Your daily tick marks will start to build up gradually, and over time, you will come to feel proud of that row of ticks and not want to ruin it by missing one. You won't want to "break the chain."

Whether you use this approach or not, the point is that you should write goals that are immediate and simple. Meanwhile, you can let the overarching objective "take care of itself."

Is Your Goal Too Ambitious?

There's nothing wrong with an ambitious goal. Many people say that "dreaming big" can make you more likely to accomplish your aim because it attracts attention, gravitates people toward you, and helps get people on board. If you tell people you want to fly to space, you will get a lot more positive attention than if you tell people you want to climb Stone Mountain (a quartz monzonite dome formation just outside Atlanta, Georgia).

Therefore, another piece of advice that often gets thrown around is for you to "have visions, not goals." Visions are abstract, and they are grand. These are things you visualize and dream about, rather than things you write down and tick off. If you want to get into shape, your goal can be to train three times a week, but your vision would be to become the best physical specimen you can – attractive to everyone and full of confidence and energy.

BUT WHILE A VISION can be as grand and extreme as you like, those smaller steps should still be small, and they should be easy. At least at the very start, your plan should be easy, and this will then allow you to build towards your higher overarching objective. Think of this as a pyramid. At the top, you have your grand vision for the future – something so exciting that it helps you to launch yourself out of bed in the morning. Beneath that, you might have your 'realistic' version of what you can achieve with your current resources. Beneath that, you might have the steps you are taking every day to achieve it.

MANY PEOPLE MAKE a mistake to lump all these things together and not consider the necessary sequencing required to move from one level to the next. Lumping is why someone who has never been to the gym before might well write themselves a new training program that requires them to train for an hour a day, seven days a week, and to do this on a diet of 1,000 calories. Is it any wonder that they don't tend to stick to their plan and fail to reach their goals?

IMPATIENCE IS your enemy when it comes to writing good goals. People want to accomplish their goals now. They don't want to put in the time or the repetitious work that it takes to reach their goals. And they certainly don't want the fear that comes from the uncertainty that they might not achieve their goals after all their work.

· · ·

BUT IT WOULD HELP if you changed that thinking. Everything worth having comes with work and diligence, and this is often highly repetitive and boring. If you want to get into shape, you need to train regularly, and it takes years to get to a point where your new physique is impressive and permanent. If you want to start your own business after college, well, then there is a ton you need to learn before you even get going. Procrastinating on a goal is just as bad, by the way – which is another reason it is so important you have a clear plan of action!

A GOOD WAY TO understand this process is to look at the world of video gaming. Video games begin with a few incredibly easy levels to prevent you from getting discouraged quickly and quitting. Craft your goals the same way – if your "level one" is a massive, difficult battle, then you won't be successful.

LET'S LOOK AT RUNNING. Lots of people get it wrong when they are taking up running for the first time. Here, they aim to start running long distances right away and losing weight. It's grueling, painful, and unrewarding, and it leaves them gasping and achy for days after.

WHAT THEY SHOULD DO IS to first focus on getting good at running and on learning to like running. That means running short distances, not running too fast, not running too far, and generally not pushing themselves beyond a sensible point. This way, they can gradually start to like running, and they can gradually find themselves running further and further without even trying.

· · ·

OFTEN, it only takes small changes to get to the place you want to be. The Japanese notion of "Kaizen" best exemplifies the impact of small changes. Kaizen essentially means lots of small changes that build up to significant results.

FOR INSTANCE, if you want to graduate with a 3.7 or higher GPA, then it might be easier to look at small changes you can make to get there rather than massive ones.

- Go to class every day.
- Create note cards after each lecture.
- Make sure you get 7 hours of sleep every night.
- Commit to the use of your daily planner.
- Visit your professors during their office hours.

THESE ARE ONLY a few minor adjustments that should be simple enough for most students to make. Still, they can have a significant impact on your overall GPA, eventually leading to a cumulative GPA of 3.7 or higher!

ONCE YOU'VE ESTABLISHED your objectives, it's a good idea to split them down into smaller steps or sub-objectives. It allows you to take modest steps forward while reducing procrastination.

OBTAINING A COLLEGE DIPLOMA, for example, can be divided into four sub-goals. The successful completion of one year of your program is the sub-goal for each of the sub-goals. Individual courses within each year can be broken down further into these sub-goals. Within the 16 weeks of lessons in each semester, the courses can be split down into tests, exams, and term papers, among other things. Each week is divided into days, with each day divided into the hours and minutes you'll spend in class and on assignments.

WHILE THINKING about all of the activities that will earn that college degree may seem overwhelming at first. Breaking down your goals into smaller chunks helps to reinforce the idea that there is a connected path connecting what you do today and the successful completion of your degree. Seeing these links can aid in tracking your development and determining whether or not you are on track. Now is a good time to think about your objectives and break them down into smaller portions.

PRO TIP – Many students struggle with goal-setting, which is understandable given that they have their entire lives ahead of them and that their objectives will shift over time. The objective is to choose goals that will provide you with the most possibilities and open up the most doors in the future.

A MARKETING DEGREE, for example, will provide you with more alternatives than a degree in Ancient Animal Bite Marks if all other factors are equal. When in doubt, select the course that will give you the most possibilities in the future.

PLEASE VISUALIZE the steps you'll take to achieve your goals now that you've established a list of them. Visualizing the measures you'll take to achieve your objectives boosts your chances of succeeding. Successful athletes practice how they will perform in a game repeatedly in their heads so that when game day arrives, they will be at their best. You can directly apply the strategy to any goal you want to achieve using the athletes' prior expertise.

MANY STUDENTS MAKE the mistake of focusing so intently on achieving their objective or the end state reward that they overlook the importance of enjoying their college experience. Many students rush to graduate and begin their professions that they do not make the most of their time in school. We appreciate life more when we are satisfied with our current efforts rather than fantasizing about how wonderful it will be when we reach our long-term goal.

FOR EXAMPLE, rather than just surviving the ride till we reach our goal, we will enjoy a road trip more if we opt to take an interest in the sights along the way. Similarly, rather than accomplishing the bare minimum to pass a class, we enjoy it more when we investigate the topic beyond what is required.

DON'T CREATE unreasonable goals or have too many ambitions to achieve. This is something that many students undertake early in the semester. When they discover they don't have enough time or energy to achieve their objectives, they quickly feel disappointed. Recognizing our physical, mental, and emotional limitations is vital for creating realistic goals, and school life is about more than just receiving that diploma or certificate.

Change your Mindset

While some individuals will almost surely be envious when you begin to achieve your objectives, you will most likely face your greatest challenge from within. Young adults are typically their own worst enemies, and as we start to achieve success, some primal defense mechanism kicks in. Our mind starts telling us all these insane things – which we usually believe because, hey, we're scared and afraid.

THE TRUTH IS that we have reservations about almost everything we encounter on our way to achievement. Successful people have trained their thoughts to be helpful rather than critical, and while it takes some time, you can truly train your mind to get out of your own way. Here are some techniques to ensure that you are approaching your goals with the appropriate mindset.

1. **Believe in Success:** We all have moments when we tell ourselves that we don't deserve to be happy for whatever reason. Perhaps it stems from shame or a lack of belief in our own worthiness to be happy and achieve our objectives. If your mind is telling you that you don't deserve the kind of success you want, remind yourself that it is a lie. Believe in yourself and your ability to succeed and be happy. We all deserve it, but few are ready to put up the effort required to obtain it.

2. **Develop Confidence in Yourself:** Confidence is a tremendous tool; when you have it, you are practically unstoppable; nevertheless, when you don't have it, it might be difficult to achieve anything. You can accomplish your objectives. You have

the intelligence, the drive, the attitude, and the capacity to succeed. You have everything you need to achieve your goals. You must first put forth the effort; belief will come as a result.

3. Don't Think in Extremes: Thinking in extremes - both positively and negatively – can be one of life's biggest roadblocks. We tend to think in extremes: up/down, on/off, success/failure, happy/sad, and so on. Of course, none of these extremes are absolute, but standing on the verge of anything makes it difficult to be objective about the complete spectrum of possibilities. Don't get caught up in thinking about your successes and failures in terms of extremes.

4. Don't Overgeneralize: Sometimes,, we all can be drama queens when something terrible happens. We say things like,, "Oh, I'll never be able to achieve this goal." Negative thought processes are one of the worst mistakes you can make. Saying things like: "I must be the worst person ever to try this, I am not smart like other students." is a recipe for long and difficult life. Setbacks are going to happen, and sometimes you are going to fail. It's not the end of the world, and you're probably doing better than a lot of people. Don't overgeneralize; try to look at things objectively, and most importantly, keep going.

5. Celebrate Your Success: When you reach one of your daily, weekly, monthly, or yearly goals, don't minimize it. Achieving any goal is a big deal. Every single time you reach a goal – even if it's nothing more than your daily progress update – you are building momentum. Keep going and keep meeting those goals because you'll be achieving your dreams before you know it.

Goals - A Final Thought

As you can see, learning to structure your goals correctly and having the right mindset can make a big difference in your likelihood of accomplishing your goals. The key is to set your sights high but to have concrete, small steps that you can take along the way to get there. Don't focus on how long it will take, deal with it being "boring," and focus on repeating the same few actions every day until you eventually achieve the thing you want to achieve or become the person you want to become.

IF YOU ASSESS the situation in the future after you have gained more experience and knowledge, you can rethink your approach again. Like anything else, this approach takes time, practice, and effort. In time, you will find things that work for you and things that don't work. You should make adjustments to your process as you gain more knowledge and experience!

NOW THAT YOU have your goals in mind, the next step is walking the road toward achieving them. Achievement begins with understanding our time. Let's explore how to become aware of the time you have available to you.

2

SMALL CHANGES...BIG IMPACT

Where Did My Day Go?

Have you ever looked at the time and thought, wow, it's 3:00 pm already, where did my day go? We have all been there at one point or another, but the first key to managing your time is to understand where your time gets spent. One very helpful way of determining where your time goes is to start tracking your time. The process here is similar to making a schedule, but it works in reverse. Instead of writing things down that you are planning to do, time logging is a process of writing down the things that you have already done. Doing this is sort of a get-to-know yourself exercise because this practice will highlight many of the habits that you might not even realize are eating big chunks of your time.

FOR INSTANCE, some people find that they watch a YouTube video or two before starting on their work every time they plan to do some classwork. That five or ten minutes a day can add up to days of lost study time over just one semester. Instead of studying for that English test, they check their social networks and update their friends that they will be offline for a few hours, which of course, leads to a few quick interactions from well-wishing friends. Other people can't seem to find the motivation to get started, to find their focus, and they find ways to procrastinate endlessly until the very last minute when anxiety finally fuels action.

WHATEVER YOUR CURRENT time management habits, time tracking will help you adjust and fine-tune your time management practices. Having accurate information about your time usage patterns is the foundation for forming good time management habits. The following are a few of my favorite recommendations to help you track your time. Please don't skip this exercise. Take the time to do this – it will truly open your eyes and help you take control of your time.

1. Time tracking is not as complex as it might first seem. At the end of every hour, make a note about how you spent your time for that hour. The note needn't be long - one sentence or less should suffice. If how you spent your time doesn't match an already planned activity, enter a comment as to what you did during that time. This way, you will be able to review patterns that emerge in your time use and make adjustments to improve your productivity.

2. Many people find it helpful to modify their planning page to facilitate tracking time. The modifications are easy enough: make two columns on your paper for each day of the week. In one column, write down the activity you are trying to achieve; in the second column, make notes on what you did with your

time. The side-by-side comparison is very revealing and an excellent way to figure out where you're not using time in the way you intend.

3. Another effective way to make changes and get results from your time management strategies is to summarize your time use by a time category such as sleep, study, work, travel, etc.

BEFORE DOING THE SUMMARY, make a sheet with different columns for each category. Your log sheet might look something like this:

ACTIVITY
Expected Time
Actual Time
Variance

STUDY FOR MATH Test
3-hours
5-hours
-2 hours

REVIEW ENGLISH NOTES
2-hours
1-hours
+1 hour

READ BOOK CHAPTER

1-hour
1-hour
0 hours

Work on Industry Paper

2-hours
3-hours
-1 hour

Group Study Session

2-hours
1-hours
+1 hour

Sleep

8-hours
5-hours
+3 hours

Night Out

4-hours
7-hours
-3 hours

Total
22 hours
23 hours
-1 hour

Estimate the amount of time you think you spend on the

various activities listed and enter these in the "expected" row of the summary sheet. Feel free to add any additional categories that might be helpful. Then log your time for one week on an hour-by-hour basis. When the week is over, summarize your time by category for each day, add up the values for all seven days of the week, and write the totals in the "actual" row of the summary sheet.

SUMMARIZING your time use allows you to understand how much time you spend in the various areas of your life. It is almost certain that you will see a notable difference between the number of hours you expected to use in certain categories and the actual number of hours you spend.

IF YOU FIND that you spend more time in one area than you wanted and less in another, the weekly summary of time used indicates which activities to reduce to find the extra time you want for that neglected area of your life.

THE DIFFERENCES between your expected use of time and your actual use of time represent your opportunities for improvement. These differences are where your focus should be. You need to identify and adjust the patterns in your behavior that are creating these variances. Small changes can make an enormous impact over time and greatly aid you in reaching your goals. These small changes, when taken together, drive a compound effect allowing you to achieve huge rewards from a series of small but intelligent choices.

. . .

THE REASON this approach goes relatively unnoticed by the masses is that these small changes seem to make no immediate impact, no obvious impact, they don't seem to matter.   Most people can't understand the cumulative effect that these small positive changes can create in their lives. They miss that these seemingly minor adjustments taken consistently over time will create significant differences. Let me give you a few examples of the power of small actions compounding over time featured in Darren Hardy's Bestselling book, The Compound Effect.

The Magic Penny

If you had a choice between taking $3 million in cash today or a single magic penny that would double in value every day for the next 31 days, which choice would you pick? If you've heard this parable before, you know the magic penny is your most profitable choice. But why is it so difficult to believe choosing the magic penny is the best choice in the long run? The basic reason is that we are programmed to believe that it takes large significant actions to make any difference in our lives. Also, our brains believe anything that takes long periods to deliver a result is painful and pushes us in the direction of immediate fun and gratification.   Fun always seems to trump long-term commitment. Let's look at our magic penny example.

FOR THE SAKE OF DISCUSSION, let's say you took the $3 million in cash, and your friend decides to take a flyer on that magic penny. On Day Seven, your friend has sixty-four cents. You, however, still have $3 million, less, of course, some of those fancy purchases you made. On Day Fourteen, your friend is up to a whopping $81.92. Not looking too good for your friend at this point! You have been enjoying your millions and watching your friend struggle with only pennies to show for it.

. . .

AFTER 21 DAYS, with only ten days left in our story, the magic penny has only generated $10,486. For all your friend's sacrifice, she has barely more than $10,000. You, however, have been enjoying a $3 million windfall. On Day Twenty-Seven the magic penny has only generated a paltry $671,088. You are thrilled with your decision to take the $3 million. But then the seemingly poor-performing magic penny starts to gain steam, and the compound effect's power starts to take hold. That same power of that seemingly ill-advised doubling magic penny, that small doubling each day, takes hold and makes that magic penny worth $10,737,418.24 on Day Thirty-one, more than three times your $3 million.

WHAT DO you think about your choice now? This parable is meant to demonstrate the power of small actions taken consistently over time is surprisingly powerful. On day Twenty-nine, you've got your $3 million; the magic penny has about $2.7 million. It isn't until that 30th day that your friend pulls ahead with $5.3 million. And it isn't until the 31st day that your friend blows your doors off; she ends up with a whopping $10,737,418.24 compared to your now seemly small $3 million.

VERY FEW THINGS are as powerful as the "magic" of compounding actions taken consistently over time. Not surprisingly, this "magic force" is equally powerful in all areas of your life.

BETTER CHOICES, reinforced with positive habits, applied consistently over time, is the key to happiness and success in life. The sooner you realize that the habits that drive your actions are compounding your life into either success or failure, the better off you will be. The good news is that tiny, small adjustments applied to your daily routines can dramatically change your trajectory and lead to the success you desire in your life. Once more, I'm not talking about massive quantum leaps of change or a complete renovation of your life. Just like the magic penny, seemingly minor changes can and will transform everything.

The Lost Plane

Another illustration of how a seemingly minor unnoticeable change can impact your goals is the story of an airplane traveling from Los Angeles to New York City. If the plane is a mere one percent off course leaving Los Angeles, with no course corrections in route, the plane will ultimately end up about 150 miles off target, arriving either in Dover Delaware or Upstate in Albany, New York. Just like a small one percent error leads to the plane missing its intended goal, so it is with your habits. One single poor habit, which doesn't look like much on the surface, can ultimately lead to you finding yourself miles from your goals and dreams.

FOR THOSE OF you now freaked out by the thought of not knowing exactly where you spend your time, here's something to consider. We all have 168 hours available in a week. Studies report that fully half of those 168 hours – 84 hours - are used up for the "basics" like sleeping, eating, showering, etc. How do your numbers compare to these estimates? How will you spend those critical remaining 84 hours per week?

3

MANAGE YOUR TIME, MANAGE YOUR LIFE

Y ou have no prior experience arranging for your out-of-class coursework as a student. A decent rule of thumb is to plan two to three hours of schoolwork outside of class for every hour spent in class. Yes, this means that a full-time student with five classes and a regular fifteen-hour class load per week should set aside between thirty and forty-five hours per week for study/homework.

SURE, this is a significant amount of time, especially if you breezed through high school on much less. This estimate is based on the amount of time it takes to learn well at the college level. You can alter your anticipated times up or down depending on the complexity of each of your lessons. As I previously indicated, you spent around 80% of your time learning in school in high school and only 20% of your time learning outside of school. The ratio has now been reversed in college, posing a new challenge for you as a college student. Only approximately a quarter of your learning occurs in class, and the other eighty percent takes place outside of it.

· · ·

THE TRANSITION from a highly regimented high school to a largely unstructured college setting necessitates a whole new approach to your academic career. The goal is to dedicate this time solely to learning and then adapt as needed based on your experience and outcomes.

IF YOU HAVE a job and it isn't necessarily preventing you from succeeding in school, you'll need to think about your work schedule and arrange some time for yourself each week. A good beginning point would be 10 percent of your week or seventeen hours. More important than particular goals is spending enough time on education to succeed and enough time outside of school to maintain a healthy balance.

MAKE sure you leave room in your daily agenda for unplanned disruptions. Allowing some vacant spaces in your day allows you to be flexible enough to deal with disruptions or unexpected demands on your time. If the unexpected does not occur, there will be enough time to accomplish something else.

MANY STUDENTS DISCOVER that scheduling schoolwork earlier in the day reduces the likelihood of being interrupted by unforeseen circumstances. Every day's schedule should include homework. In a comprehensive study on stress, students claimed that doing homework was the most common strategy for alleviating stress in their lives.

· · ·

THAT MAY SEEM strange to you, but getting ahead of the curve and finishing your homework will reduce your stress levels because you won't have that activity hanging over your head all of the time.

REMEMBER that rather than a big list of "have-to-dos," your daily calendar should contain at least some time for doing what you want to accomplish. Looking forward to something every day is beneficial to our mental health and can help us avoid burnout.

WHEN WE LOOK at our schedule on some days, it can feel daunting. If this is the case, focusing on one activity at a time and avoiding looking at the entire day can be beneficial. You'll be surprised at how swiftly you complete the day's activities.

YOU'LL HAVE to make changes to your plans and time management habits sooner or later. Keep in mind that certain time problems are predictable, while others are not; some are controlled, while others are not. Keep your cool and get back on track as soon as possible if you can't control it. Deal with time problems that you can control, especially those that occur regularly, immediately and quickly, so they don't get in the way of your goals.

SELF-CONTROL IS REQUIRED for time management. It takes time, but time management becomes an everyday habit after a short period of self-management.

- Be conscious of how you spend your time.

- Don't put off doing tasks and don't wait until the last minute to do assignments and projects.
- Allow enough time in your day to do things you enjoy, as well as eat and sleep. Sleep deprivation is a widespread issue on most college campuses.
- Make the most of your time. If you're on the bus or shuttle, make time to read while you're on the road.

STAYING one day ahead is one of the most effective time management tactics. I'm sure this remark will elicit some collective moans, but trust me when I say that keeping exactly one day ahead of your classes will make your life a lot simpler, especially when that sickness circulating campus takes the wind out of your sails.

YOUR LECTURERS WILL MOST likely offer you one of the most crucial pieces of information you will ever get — the syllabus — at the start of most of your classes. You probably never received a syllabus in high school. You had no idea what the reading or homework assignment for the next two weeks would entail. You do it in college. What is the significance of this? It's the secret to mastering your time management.

LET'S assume it's the first day of school. You receive your biology course syllabus. In most circumstances, the first day of class is a no-brainer; often, the lecturer skips the material lecture because they know that many students will quit or add classes that first week. You take a look at your handy syllabus and notice that the next class time will consist of a lecture on the first chapter of your $199.99 textbook. "Wait a minute," you might think at this vital moment "Oh, I've already decided what I'm going to do next class period. I'm not sure if this is genuinely useful information. Is it possible for me to take advantage of this?"

MANY STUDENTS TOSS the golden ticket of the syllabus into their backpack, fold it into a paper aircraft, or come up with another creative use for these sheets of paper, and then do nothing until the next class hour.

WHEN THE NEXT class period arrives two days later, you haven't read chapter one, but who cares, because your professor will talk about it. You figure that you will use the time-honored tradition of taking notes in class. After all, everyone's doing it.

BUT SUPPOSE you're spending all of your time trying to copy PowerPoint slides or copy written words on the board (your professor will most likely have handwriting that resembles some ancient language). In that case, you simply aren't going to absorb the material in most cases.

LET'S say you take some great notes - good for you! Then you take the notes, which have all of the information you will ever need, and you put them in your folder, binder, backpack, or saddle-pack, and leave them there until the next lecture. Then you take more notes, add them to the pile, and soon have lots of notes. Whoopee.

. . .

BEFORE YOU KNOW IT, you have a test or quiz approaching, so you assemble your nifty notes and start restudying them like mad. You have to set apart a large chunk of time out of your schedule to review this old information so that it will be fresh in your mind for the test.

THERE IS A BETTER WAY. Now, let's pretend that you decided to get one day ahead. After your first-class period (and I know this is hard to do because there's so much fun to be found during the first week and so little work to do), you have a heart-to-heart with yourself and decide that you will get one day ahead.

IF TODAY'S MONDAY, and the next class is Wednesday, you set aside some time on Monday afternoon or anytime on Tuesday and read the first chapter. You may even decide to take some notes, highlight, or even make notecards for definitions (more on notecards later).

WHEN YOU WALK into class on Wednesday, and your teacher starts talking, you have at least some idea and understanding around the lecture. You don't have to copy down definitions you've already read because you know they are in the book -- you remember reading them. Instead of frantically copying notes like your poor confused classmates, you can relax and make a small tick mark to denote what the professor discussed and listen to what the professor is saying.

THE LECTURE BECOMES your review session, and then you are in a much better position when test time comes. If the professor starts talking about something you don't remember reading in the textbook, take good notes. The topic is either not covered in the book (so you can guarantee the professor will put it on a test), or it's something that you didn't quite absorb the first time you read it.

IF YOU CAN DO this for each of your classes at the beginning of school, you will be in great shape. Once you get one day ahead, you can work at the same pace as everyone else, but always be a day ahead. Lectures will not be "note cramming sessions"; they'll be pseudo-reviews.

THE TOUGHEST PART is not getting lazy and letting that one-day buffer disappear. You can't let yourself slip behind because you know you're ahead. Once you lose that day, it's much harder to get it back in the middle of the semester because the pace of your classes will be picking up. If you can get ahead in that first week, the load will be much lighter.

OF COURSE, there are exceptions to every rule. Not every class is equal in difficulty, and it may be extremely hard to get that one-day edge in certain complex classes or in classes that depend almost 100% on lecture material that doesn't come from a textbook.

SOME CLASSES MAY BE JUST PLAIN hard, and if you can't get a day ahead in one or two classes, that's fine. The time that you save by being ahead in your other classes will help you enormously in that tough calculus class you're taking.

·   ·   ·

IF YOU FIND that reading your book is not helping you grasp the material, then talk to your professor. If they learn that you are trying to stay a day ahead, besides the inevitable brownie points that will follow, they will be willing to help you out. Professors are generally willing to bend over backward for any student putting out a serious effort to succeed in their class.

LET me mention that you may have some classes in which the professor has put together a "notes packet" containing copies of all the presentations and notes for that class. Be very careful not to depend solely on these notes, as this could be a trap. Don't let those notes become an excuse to get lazy. Don't think that the class lecture doesn't matter because you have all the material, get one day ahead in the class notes, and again, all of the lectures will be your review sessions.

Putting the System into Action

Keeping a calendar is pretty straightforward, but surprisingly I have discovered most students don't keep one their first semester or two. If they do keep one, it is usually just a class schedule with locations, so they know when and where to go until they get their routine committed to memory.

I WILL OFFER you some advice that seems counter-intuitive and conflicts with what most experts will tell you.   First, let me say I am a fan of technology and using your Outlook, iPhone, or Google Calendar as a way to track your activities as most experts recommend. Still, I want this to be your secondary source of scheduling, not your primary.

.   .   .

I RECOMMEND USING AN EXCEL SPREADSHEET, a DayMinder GC520 or similar planner, and your automated calendar during your first two semesters.   I know this might sound like overkill, but the idea here is not to enter events and assignments into a calendar but to develop a system that keeps you organized and on track.

AFTER A COUPLE OF SEMESTERS, you will find the system, and the process will have become a habit and will be natural for you.

LET'S look at how all these approaches work together, and everything will become clear.

FIRST DAY/WEEK of the Semester

THE FIRST THING I want you to do is to take your syllabi from each class and markdown (in pencil) all your assignments for the semester in your DayMinder, don't forget mid-term and final exams).

NOW USE different color highlighters for each class (Math, English, Communications, etc.) and highlight your assignments in your planner.

NEXT, identify areas where you have multiple assignments, test, exams, etc. all clustered together in a particular week or day. These clusters allow you to see clearly up front where you will

be stressed and have little time.   Like most students, you will
see a convergence around spring and fall breaks and the last
month of the semester. Take a deep breath, and don't panic!

Now we want to pay attention to the weights of our assignments. Review your syllabi for each class and underline in red
in your planner all your significant assignments.   Significant is
a subjective term, and each class will vary, but in general,
anything weighted 10% of your grade or higher will qualify.

Once we have our core class schedule, we have to make some
study estimates.   Use two hours of study time for each hour of
class time as a baseline requirement for scheduling your week.
Adjust this baseline up or down based on your comfort and the
difficulty of your class material. If you struggle with Math, you
should bump up your baseline to 3 hours. If you are an English
expert, you can adjust the baseline down to 1 hour or maybe 1.5
hours.   We now want to schedule our study time right into
your planner.   Planning a specific study schedule is key to
avoiding procrastination.   If you work or play sports and have
that weekly commitment, schedule it now. Keep track of your
study and assignment hours so that you can make adjustments
throughout the semester.

Things are probably starting to look pretty crowded at this
point, and you are beginning to wonder where all that free time
you heard about will show up.   Don't worry; by planning, you
will maximize your free time.

·   ·   ·

NOW WE WANT to identify the areas on your calendar where you have little or no assignments due. Highlight these areas in Green in your DayMinder. We will utilize these areas to pull forward work you previously underlined in red and the areas where you have lots of things converging. Look for those large significant assignments and break them down into smaller chunks with new due dates you create for yourself. These are called milestones. By utilizing these green areas, you will balance your workload to reduce future stress and have the time available to do your best work.

IF YOU KNOW you are going to go out with your friends on Friday and Saturday nights, make sure you schedule that time as well. If you will be out to the early morning hours and then sleep in until 2 pm, plan for that. Be realistic and don't set yourself up to fail by scheduling 4 hours of study time every Saturday morning when you already know you will be sleeping until early afternoon.

NOW THAT WE have everything organized and scheduled, we can enter everything into our online or smartphone calendars and set up our alert notifications. The electronic calendar now keeps us on schedule, but our pre-planning ensures we effectively utilize our time.

I RECOMMEND that students get one day ahead in their classes as soon as possible, things happen, schedules change, etc., but by building in a day buffer, you are preparing for that unplanned event that will inevitably occur at some point during the semester.

. . .

ALSO, class syllabi are guidelines, and the due dates and assignments will change in many instances. You will want to make sure you prepare for that new last-minute paper the professor decided to throw at you in the last month of classes. Yes, it happens more often than you would like. A professor will feel that the class isn't picking up on something as a whole or that something new has happened in the field, and the professor will decide to add an assignment to strengthen your academic foundation. He or She may feel like the class has not engaged or participated as well as they should have, or they may want to allow everyone to improve their grades. Regardless, you want to be prepared.

ALSO, schedule a time to Skype or call your family or someone else important to you back home. You will be surprised at how fast the days can run together, and although you are probably texting frequently, your loved ones love to hear your voice and see your face.

THIS TEMPLATE IS straightforward to use and will summarize all your activities for you in one place (see table 1). In the tab, you merely enter your activities on the Class List and Activities Tab (see table 2) classes, study time, practices, clubs, events, etc., in the tab, and the spreadsheet will organize everything for you.

TABLE 1: Time Management Schedule

TABLE 2: Time Management Activities

EACH WEEK – Review and Plan

PICK a day each week to review the week and month ahead. Most students find Sundays work best for this review. Remember to schedule calendar review time and treat this time like you would any other required commitment. Log into your universities course management system and review your upcoming assignment lists for any changes or assignments you may have missed. As a side note, make sure you confirm all assignments you turned in are showing as turned in. Every semester students think they turned in an assignment, but the system will say otherwise. It is your responsibility to make sure your assignment was submitted and received. Use this time to clean up your email inbox and check and see if any of your professors have made schedule changes for the week ahead. The critical activity in this weekly review is to establish the specific activities and work you will perform during your allotted time slots. Initially, we just blocked off the time we knew we would need. Once we have the specifics, we can now schedule the activities and tasks we need to complete during the week. As an example, we can take the 3 hours we have scheduled to study for a particular class and break down how we will use those three hours. Are we going to review note cards, read a chapter in the text, work on a paper, etc.?

DAILY

EACH DAY BEFORE NOON, review your next day's schedule and school email account. If something new has popped up, you forgot about something, etc.. By checking the next day's activities and your email early enough, you leave yourself time to course-correct if needed. Many students check their next day's calendar just before going to bed. If they have made a mistake or missed something, they have no time to correct their error, stress levels rise, they don't sleep, and the next day's performance suffers. Students often don't get emails sent to their university accounts regularly, so they can get out of the habit of periodically checking their school email and miss valuable information such as assignments or cancellations of classes.

THE BIG PICTURE

MOST STUDENTS STRUGGLE WITH STRUCTURE, and that is natural. By creating a schedule, you are not somehow magically sucking all the fun out of your life. You are reducing your stress and improving your performance, allowing you to enjoy yourself a whole lot more. You will miss study sessions and other events on your calendar... that's ok. It is very valuable to know you missed an event and not go around fooling yourself into thinking you are on track. If you miss something, ask if you can make it up. You would be surprised how many students just assume the professor will not cut them a break. Make sure you identify what caused you to veer off course, make adjustments, and learn from the experience.

Creating Balance in Your Life

With everything that is going on in life, you need a simple system to make sure you have time for school, work, and fun. Yes, you're in college to get an education and gain the skill you need for a successful career, but you are also here to have fun, create new experiences, and hopefully, a few lifelong friends.

THERE IS A VERY simple technique you can use to make sure you keep your life in balance, a technique called *The Eisenhower Matrix or Eisenhower Box*. By utilizing this prioritization approach, you will be able to balance your hectic college life.

THIS TECHNIQUE IS NAMED after former President Dwight D. Eisenhower, the top general in World War II. He is credited with many accomplishments in his life, including leading the allied forces to victory, developing the Interstate Highway System, and spearheading the creation of NASA. As a General and a President, he was widely regarded as extremely effective and organized. We all can learn a lot from President Eisenhower, so let's take a look at how he could accomplish so much.

PRESIDENT EISENHOWER WAS famous for saying, "What is important is seldom urgent, and what is urgent is seldom important."

. . .

THE MATRIX CONSISTS of a square divided into four sections or quadrants. Here's how the four quadrants are laid out:

WE START by placing all our activities into the four quadrants, with the labels of Important and Urgent on each side. Each quadrant has a value of 1 through 4 based on their current priority.

1. "IMPORTANT" and "Urgent" tasks. These are all your level 1 priorities. If you have an exam the next day, studying is probably a top priority. Paper due tomorrow, again, a level 1 activity, connect assignment due tomorrow, another level 1 priority. Level 1 priorities are those things with immediate deadlines, things that will make the most impact on your goals and vision, and these activities should grab your immediate attention.

2. "IMPORTANT," but "Not Urgent" tasks. These are things still aligned with your goals and vision, but there is no immediate deadline staring you in the face. Maybe it is doing some extra reading on a topic in your major, attending a seminar before graduation, or reviewing your 4-year plan. You will work on these tasks whenever you have a lull in your schedule.

3. "NOT IMPORTANT," but "Urgent" tasks. These are things that you will complete after your level 1 priorities are complete or delegate altogether. Can your roommate check out that journal from the library for you? Could a friend pick up your toothpaste from the store for you? Maybe your parents need some information from you, or a friend needs a little help?

. . .

4. **"Not Important" and "Not Urgent" tasks.** These are the activities you put in quadrant 4 or activities you should eliminate. Do you really need to binge-watch Season 3 of "Orange is the New Black," or should you work on your quadrant 2 activities?

THE UNDERLYING VALUE in this matrix is its simple ability to compare activities, which are really urgent and really important. Urgent activities require your immediate attention; important activities help you with your long-term goals.

THE EISENHOWER MATRIX

Organization Matters

Usually, college students aren't quite prepared to organize all the "stuff" in their lives as they transition to college. Dorm rooms can quickly get overrun with stuff like clothes, books, computers, mini-fridges, microwaves, television sets, and the other possessions of the college student's life.

. . .

EVEN IF YOU'RE going to college locally and still living at home in the same room you've been in since you were a child, you still need to make room for the new trappings of college life. Try a few of these organizational tips.

YOU WILL NEED a few supplies to get you started. First, you will need colored file folders, a portable plastic file holder, some colored binders, a 3-hole punch, and a few small bins that will get you started.

DESIGNATE ONE COLOR for each class and store pending assignments in them as you work on them. Place these folders inside the plastic holder. Be sure to write on the tab which class each folder is for to ease identification. You can also use the file folder approach to store important papers and receipts.

THE COLORED BINDERS are used for each class to store all the papers you receive in that class. As we talked about earlier, you will get a syllabus – put this in the front. Then, whenever you get a handout from your professor, place it in the binder. Use section dividers to label what information corresponds with which section. You should also keep completed assignments in this binder for easy referral, and in case your instructor "loses" one of your grades – then you can prove you did the work! It does happen, especially when your professor is handling hundreds of student assignments at any given time. Also, a professor may easily overwrite or enter a grade in the system wrong. Having an organized method to keep your assignments will make your life much easier when you sit down with your professor to review the mistake. You would be shocked to learn the number of times a student reaches out to me the last few weeks of the semester and asks for a copy of their initial assignment outlines, so they can get back to work on the project they were supposed to be working on all semester. Don't do this; it won't end well.

KEEP an ample supply of pens and #2 pencils on hand, and use the bins for small items you accumulate like paper clips, push pins for a bulletin board, stapler, etc. It's a good idea to keep extra supplies like printer paper and printer cartridges – just in case!

NOW THAT YOU have the tools let's make sure you stay organized. Assignments can disappear in a pile of paper. Textbooks can get lost within a mound of laundry. A cluttered dorm room creates stress! Disorganization is all around us and happens practically everywhere, even in the most scholarly of places, like a college campus. But, there is an easy solution.

THE RULE with paper is very simple. There are only three things you can do with paper:

1. Act on it
2. File it
3. Toss it

FOR EXAMPLE, if you get a piece of mail, open it. Don't create a huge clutter problem by letting unopened mail pile up. You must decide what to do with your opened mail. If it is a catalog or a piece of junk mail and you know that you will not use it, toss it. Pay it, mail it, or file it in a "bills due" folder if it is a bill. If you receive a memo or note after reading it, toss it or file it away. If you get a paper returned, file it away. If you don't, the clutter and stress will build.

ANOTHER IMPORTANT PLACE TO de-clutter is your computer. If you can keep your files under control, you won't be looking in 20 different folders in "My Documents" for that English paper you wrote last week. Here are some suggestions to get rid of computer clutter.

- Deleting or archiving any e-mail you read will keep your inbox clean.
- Create a filing system- if you cannot reply right away or need to save an e-mail, place it in a folder made for that category. (Needs Reply, or Archives)
- Watch your "sent mail" folder. Delete or archive things from that as well.
- Add to your address book often. Many times, people will keep an e-mail in their inbox so that they have the address for the future. Instead of that, save the address. You'll know where to find it later.
- Utilize spam filters on your e-mail account to limit inbox distractions. Just don't forget to check your junk and spam mail folder for things that slipped through.
- Setting up folders by semester will keep your "My Documents" folder easier to navigate, as well as allow for quick reference.
- Move files to Dropbox or another backup device as a standard course of business. You don't want to lose any work, and routinely backing up your work

in case of failure can save you untold time and stress.

LIKE ANY OTHER SKILL, organization is a skill that can be learned. The most difficult part is breaking your lifelong bad habits. The key to getting better organized is to start with one small step and then take additional small steps one after the other. You may find that what you've put off for days takes only a few minutes to do. And once you see the benefits in one part of your life, you'll be motivated to expand this practice.

ALL THE TIME management and organization tips in the world can only help if you put them to use. Putting things off can be the biggest mistake most students make.

I'll Stop Procrastinating Today, Well Maybe Not Today!

Procrastination is a goal buster; wait it's more than that; it's a life buster. You might be thinking, isn't that a bit dramatic? I have always procrastinated, and I have gotten along just fine! I am here to tell you, what got you here, won't get you where you want to go. You must raise your game! And if you only change one bad habit, make it to STOP procrastinating!

IT'S easy to put things off until later, especially when you dread a task such as writing a term paper. But as a student, this is a real problem. If you put off your assignments or study for tests, you are only hurting yourself. Procrastinating leads to stress and anxiety, not to mention poor performance. You CAN stop procrastination from affecting your schoolwork.

. . .

OFTEN STUDENTS SUFFER from procrastination and find it diffi-cult to get started working on their assignments. Most of the time, not starting seems to be related to stress, fear, or simply feeling overwhelmed with the whole process. Aim to subdivide tasks into small steps and convince yourself that all you need is five minutes working on the task to get started. Often, five minutes is all you'll need to get into the swing of things, and you can continue productively. I call this trick "The Five-Minute Hack."

SOMETIMES I HEAR students say they don't feel motivated to start their assignments; they are waiting for inspiration or a changing mood. I got news for you... people who wait on the mood to strike or motivation to hit them will find themselves doing everything last minute. Mood and Motivation aren't prerequisites to action...**it is a result of it!**

TRY WORKING for a short time and see if you can "get into it." If your motivation problem seems more substantial, it might help to realize that when you aren't motivated to do school work, you aren't out of motivation... **you are just motivated to do something else.**

MAKE every effort to develop the discipline you need to follow your plan. Your planner should always be handy, and you should refer to it often. Once you make your schedule, follow it. If you need help staying on task, work with a roommate or friend to motivate each other and hold each other accountable. Remind yourself you are focused on your long-term goals, and once you complete your work, you are one step closer to achieving those goals. And remember, by sticking to your plan, you will have more time for yourself.

IF YOU ARE STRUGGLING to stick to your plan, try this tip. Make two activity lists: "Things I Like to Do" and "Things I Have to Do." Mix up activities from both lists and work on each activity for a short period. Alternating between fun and work helps to maintain motivation and interest. All work and no fun is another schedule buster. You don't have to be working ALL the time, but you do have to complete what is required to stay on plan.

SOMETIMES, you're going to feel overwhelmed with large projects or assignments. Remind yourself that this is a normal reaction. When you feel like this, it's easier to put things off because you don't know exactly where to start and have difficulty envisioning the completed task. Divide these major assignments into smaller parts and work on one part at a time. Then put them together into the whole project and feel the satisfaction of a job well done!

YOU MIGHT HAVE every intention of doing things promptly, but time can move swiftly. There are only 24 hours in a day, and some people are just over aggressive with their planning. Make sure your schedule is realistic, and you aren't involved in too many activities scheduled close together. If you spread yourself too thinly, none of your projects will get the attention they deserve.

. . .

REWARD yourself when you complete tasks on time. Make the reward appropriate for the difficulty and boredom of the task. Utilizing rewards will help you stay on task and provide fuel for action.

REMEMBER that you're not alone. Some studies report that up to 95% of students experience procrastination as a real problem. Many students do most of the work in marathon sessions near academic deadlines and fail to use time management skills, tools, and study aids I recommend. Doing this leads to more stress in your already stressful life. Why add to your stress?

AT THIS POINT, you are probably wondering why people procrastinate on tasks related to goals they want to achieve? Procrastination often emerges as a means of distancing oneself from stressful activities. People allocate more time to tasks they judge as easy or fun than tasks they judge as difficult or boring. Dealing with the underlying stressful aspects of the activities can assist in reducing the extent of procrastination. We'll address the problem of stress management a little later.

PRO TIP - If the volume of work on your to-do list overwhelms you, you might benefit from making a "one-item list." Re-write the top item from your list at the top of a blank page and work the task to completion, then take the next item on your list and place that on a blank sheet, repeat the process until you complete everything on your original list.

SOME PEOPLE MUST OVERCOME procrastination gradually. Almost no one has trouble studying the night before a big exam. But without the pressure of an exam, many students find it easy to avoid studying. If you need the motivation for the looming deadline, remember to implement the five-minute hack.

THE KEY IS to learn the habit of getting started on a task early, i.e., the procrastinator needs to learn to initiate studying and preparing for papers and exams well in advance. Practice starting to study several times every day. As with exercising, getting started and making it a routine are the secrets to success. Other valuable suggestions include:

- Recognize self-defeating problems such as; fear and anxiety, difficulty concentrating, poor time management, indecisiveness, and perfectionism.
- Keep your goals in mind and identify your strengths and weaknesses, values and priorities.
- Compare your actions with the values you feel you have. Are your values consistent with your actions?
- Discipline yourself to use time wisely.
- A study session that utilizes small blocks of time with frequent breaks is more effective than studying in long uninterrupted marathon sessions. For example, you will accomplish more if you study/work in sixty-minute blocks and take frequent ten-minute breaks in between than if you study/work for two to three hours straight, with no breaks.
- Reward yourself after you complete a successful week.
- Motivate yourself to study. Focus on success, not on failure. Try to study in small groups. Break large

assignments into smaller tasks. Keep a reminder
schedule and checklist.

- Set realistic goals.
- Modify your environment: Eliminate or minimize
  noise/ distraction. Ensure adequate lighting. Have
  the necessary equipment at hand. Don't waste time
  going back and forth to get things. Don't get too
  comfortable when studying. A desk and a straight-
  backed chair are usually best (a bed is no place to
  study). Be neat! Take a few minutes to straighten
  your desk.
- Decide when you have had enough, and it's time for
  a change.
- Think about the activities that you use to
  procrastinate (email, TV, etc.) and set clear time
  limits on them.
- Set clear goals for each day (e.g., start CHEM
  problem set, do ENGL reading, finish MRKT
  chapter reading) and stick to them. Once complete,
  you are free to do whatever you like.
- Remember that serious academic stress usually
  follows procrastination.
- Recall the stress and loss of energy you felt the last
  time you had to stay up all night to write a paper or
  study for an exam. Remembering your feelings of
  anxiety can serve as an effective motivator to help
  you get started on time now.
- Know that overcoming procrastination is sometimes
  easier if you talk out strategies for change with
  someone else.

THE POMODORO TECHNIQUE

．　．　．

GETTING STARTED IS OFTEN the hardest part of any assignment, task, or project. The thought of sitting down in front of your computer for a few hours straight can cause you enough anxiety to want to head to the dentist instead. If that sounds like you have no fear, I have a solution for you. Enter the Pomodoro technique. A *Pomodoro* is simply the interval of time spent working.

THE POMODORO TECHNIQUE was originally designed as a time management technique, but it has been slightly modified to become an effective way to overcome procrastination in recent years.

THE KEY to the success of this technique is that it only requires you to focus for 20-minutes at a time. After 20-minutes you get to take a 5-minute break. When your brain knows you will reconnect to your social media, text a friend, or catch up on your email, it makes it much easier for you to engage and get started. And once started, you will build momentum, and you will be quite surprised just how much you will achieve.

TO MAKE THIS TECHNIQUE EFFECTIVE, you must be highly focused. You need to shut off your smartphone, shut off alerts on your other devices, and remove any other distractions. You need quiet, so if you have distractions that cannot be turned off, consider wearing noise reduction headphones or heading to the school library.

．　．　．

Using the Pomodoro technique, you start by deciding what the first important task is for the day (utilize the Eisenhower Matrix). Then you set a timer for 20 minutes and focus 100% on that task.

When the timer chimes, reset it for 5-minutes, get up and do some deep breathing, stretch out your body, jump on social media, whatever you want to do for 5 minutes.

Next, set the timer, jump back in for another 20-minutes and then repeat the 5- minute break. These 20- minute sprints are called a Pomodoro.

After doing four Pomodoro, you have a completed set. Now take a 20-minute break. Make sure you put a checkmark on a piece of paper or notecard after each 20-minute Pomodoro, as it is quite easy to lose track of how many Pomodoro's you have completed.

As you get into the swing of things, feel free to adjust your Pomodoro's to 25-minutes, 30-minutes, or even 2-hours.   I personally find a 2-hour Pomodoro with a 30-minutes break highly effective when I am writing books.   When grading papers, I use the 20/5 approach outlined here.   The point I want to make is that this technique is easily modified; play with the Pomodoro's to find what works best for you.

Why Procrastination Is A Nightmare

.   .   .

GOOD IDEAS TAKE TIME. Whether you are working on a small assignment or a large paper, good ideas take time to develop and come together in a well-thought-out cohesive fashion. Most written assignments in college will require you to select a topic, then spend time developing your thoughts around your ideas, revising your thoughts, and finally fine-tuning and polishing things up. If you procrastinate and wait until the last minute, you won't have time to properly go through an intellectual process required to ensure a fully reflective and developed piece of work. This approach also applies to essay questions on tests and exams. You will want to allow time to reflect on the question rather than throwing out the first idea that pops into your head.

YOU WILL LIKELY RUN **out of time.** When it comes to strict deadlines-which is just about always in your college classes-you run the risk of missing the due date if you keep putting off your work until tomorrow. And the reality is that most professors will not give you an extension except in very special circumstances. It is not that they are trying to be mean, but once they make one exception, they will have to make hundreds. If your professor accepts late assignments, a grade penalty-often as much as one-third to one-half a grade a day will apply. Just don't take the risk.

YOU MIGHT BE BEING OVERLY **dramatic.** One of the key reasons we all procrastinate is to avoid the pain associated with actually doing the task at hand. In my experience, students overestimate the pain they'll feel while completing their assignments. It's quite understandable when faced with a 15-page paper, a 25-question problem set, or 50 pages of reading, you naturally feel the task is enormous and overwhelming, and the simple thought of starting makes your stomach sick. The reality is, if you just get started on a small piece and then another small piece, then another manageable piece, etc., you will see the assignment coming together. Your fear will disappear as you build on the positive momentum you have created.

THE TASK IS PROBABLY NOT AS HARD **as you think.** The reality is that thousands of students, just like you, have completed the task at hand. It's often hard to determine at the start of an assignment just how much time it'll take you to complete the assignment-especially if the topic is unfamiliar or covers a diverse area of topics. Just get started, and you will likely find that things are not as bad as you have built them up to be.

YOU LOSE **your chance for help.** Many students will want to enlist the help of a professor or a TA. But their time is limited, and many professors only maintain office hours a few hours a week on specific days only, and not every TA is timely when it comes to getting back to students. With most students waiting to the last minute, a classic supply vs. demand problem is created, especially if the assignment is challenging, and 75% of the students have figured out they are stuck three days before the assignment is due. By starting your assignments early, you won't lose the chance to consult with the professor or TA if you have questions. Even if you get answers to your questions at the last minute, you will not have time to implement your professor or TA suggestions, which will destroy your grade. Your Professor or TA will hate taking their time and providing feed-back and suggestions to see you completely ignore their advice.

. . .

CONTRARY TO WHAT **you might believe.** You won't work better under time constraints. If you put off your work until the last minute, your work will be hurried and demonstrate the short-cuts you took due to the time pressure. This experience will likely create stress, anxiety, and even guilt for putting off the work once again. This behavior will take its toll on your sleep, energy, and mental well-being. It simply is not the best combination for your health or GPA.

YOUR WORK WILL LOOK INCOMPLETE. One of the main differences between fair, good, and excellent work is that excellent work has gone through a natural cycle of thoughts, drafts, and revisions. The paper will flow naturally and follow a well-thought-out logical sequence. When the clock is ticking and your deadline is rapidly approaching, you will skip steps in the cycle and hand in an assignment that doesn't flow properly or hit on all the key ideas or concepts. Like a bad movie, the professor will easily notice the lack of effort into your work.

YOU PLACE **yourself at a relative disadvantage.** While you're busy being busy, putting off your work for another time, some of your fellow students are getting down to business and getting started on their assignments. These students will likely raise the bar for everyone and increase the gap between excellent work, good work, and average work. Many professors will fit their grade curves to a somewhat normal distribution or even limit the percentage of students receiving an A. Most universities expect the grades in a class section to follow a somewhat normal distribution or average grade target, ensuring a class is neither difficult nor easy. The university won't talk about this in their orientations or course program guides, but rest assured, behind those pillars of knowledge and opportunity, proper course curve fitting is being discussed and expected.

THE TASK IS THE TASK. Some students think that somehow the task is going to get easier if they wait a little longer. If they give it a little more time, some miracle or inspiration will strike that will change the course of the assignment forever. Of course, this isn't going to happen; the assignment is the assignment once your professor assigns it. Get over it, and in the words of Nike, Just Do It!

LIFE HAPPENS. Anytime you have an assignment that covers some period or involves some research or builds upon lessons, there is an increased likelihood that something distracting and unexpected will arise, thus stopping or greatly slowing down your ability to complete your work. You could catch the bug spreading around campus at the speed of a viral YouTube video. You could get food poisoning from the campus cafeteria. Another professor could spring an assignment on you that requires unscheduled time, or some work or family emergency could pop up. Whatever the event, you can count on life getting in the way, and if you have properly planned and allowed some room in your schedule for these unplanned events, you will be able to deal with things and not tank your GPA.

BALANCING CLASS LOADS, assignments, work, and fun can lead to a great deal of stress for the average student. It's important to realize that this feeling is normal, and you will feel stressed with so much going on in your life. You can easily start to feel like your life is spiraling out of control, but you're not alone, and your fellow students are feeling somewhat the same way. Consider the following:

- 85% of college students reported they had felt overwhelmed by everything they had to do at some point in the past year.
- 42% of college students stated anxiety as the top concern.
- 30% of college students reported that stress had negatively affected their academic performance.
- 25% of college students reported they were taking psychotropic medication.

IN THE NEXT CHAPTER, we'll explore how to hone your ability to concentrate.

4

HONE YOUR ABILITY TO CONCENTRATE

S uccess is heavily dependent on how you focus on what you do. Whether you are doing business, studying, working, or playing sports, focusing will help you achieve your goals. Unfortunately, we have to deal with numerous distractions in the digital environment that we live in today. Today, your friend doesn't have to pay you a visit to interfere with your schedule. A simple Facebook or Twitter message can heavily affect your to-do list.

OUR LEVELS of concentration have been heavily affected by the digital space that we float in. Most of the time, we find ourselves engulfed in social networks. What we forget is that communicating through these social platforms is not on our to-do list. How many times have you found yourself checking your emails and responding to them without any awareness of how much time has passed? This is a common thing that happens to most people. Besides going through your emails, there is a high likelihood that you will open a different tab to visit social media pages. Shortly after, you wake up to realize that you have wasted more than an hour of your prime time.

IF YOU FOUND yourself nodding about the time-wasting experience mentioned above, you should not lose hope. There are recommended strategies that you can adopt to improve your concentration skills. Before looking into this matter, let's take a closer look into some of the things that sway you from concentrating on what's important.

What's Killing Your Ability to Concentrate?

Mobile Phone

THERE ARE plenty of reasons that having a mobile phone helps in effective communication. With only the touch of a button, you can send your message to millions of people out there. However, we cannot overlook the fact that these smartphones have also affected the way we work. That's not all. They have also affected the face-to-face connections that we once had before they were introduced.

MOST PEOPLE CARRY their handsets anywhere they go. A cell phone is no longer a device for communication, but it has transformed into our best friend. Frankly, there are instances where you find yourself smiling aimlessly at the messages you read from different social pages. We no longer need the physical presence of our friends. Smartphones have occupied this space.

· · ·

UNFORTUNATELY, THESE SMARTPHONES' constant vibrating and ringing derails our attention from what we should be focusing on. Instead of working or paying attention to meaningful conversations, our phones wreck our attention.

SUCH DISTRACTIONS CAN BE ELIMINATED by admitting that you should mute your phone when at work or when attending lectures. This gives your brain the ability to focus, which could eventually lead to enhanced productivity. You can find some free time to engage with your smartphone and catch up on what you missed.

NEGATIVE MENTALITY

A NEGATIVE MINDSET will also hinder your concentration. You should realize that you will be channeling your energy to worrying about things that you have no control of. We all have good and bad times. That's a fact. The last thing you should be doing is wasting your time and energy thinking about the hurdles before you.

NEGATIVITY THWARTS YOUR CREATIVITY. In the presence of negativity, you will not be as productive as you thought. Don't allow your emotions to get the best of you. Find someone you trust and talk to him or her about what you are experiencing. This will be beneficial because it creates vents to allow such negative vibes to flow away.

LACK OF SLEEP

. . .

WE ALL HAVE a story to tell when it comes to feeling sleepy during lectures. It's early in the morning, and you are struggling to keep your eyes open. This has happened to all of us at some time in our lives. Usually, this becomes a problem throughout the day. You will not study effectively since your mind is not alert.

LACK OF SLEEP has a detrimental effect on our concentration. It slows down our thought processes, making it daunting for us to focus (Schwartzbard, 2019). The effect is that you will find it challenging to complete a given task in time. There are various reasons that you might be tempted to stay up all night. For instance, if you are watching a film series, it could lure you into watching it all night. Nonetheless, it is important to stop and consider the benefit on your productivity the following day if you choose to sleep early.

MULTITASKING

ANOTHER REASON you will struggle to concentrate on what you are doing is your habit of multitasking. An interesting revelation that will strike your attention is that intelligent students don't multitask. Instead, they focus on doing one thing at a time. What's more, you ought to understand that multitasking is just a myth. The human brain cannot multitask. A perception of multitasking only does more harm than good to your brain.

. . .

RESEARCH SHOWS that when people think they are multitasking, the reality is that they are switching from one task to the other. The switch is done super quickly to the point that one thinks they are attending to multiple tasks simultaneously. Quickly switching from one activity to the other hinders optimal performance (Glowatz, 2019).

So, if you thought that you were saving time by responding to your emails while doing your homework, you need to think twice. Refrain from the urge to multitask and do one thing at a time. If there are smaller tasks that you should complete, schedule them for a later period when you are through with high-priority assignments.

Boredom

BOREDOM ALSO HAS a role to play in your lack of concentration. Unfortunately, this is something that you have no control over. There are particular occasions when you are assigned boring tasks to do. Honestly, this is unavoidable. Unfortunately, there are times when you just want to avoid what you are doing so that you don't feel bored with the task at hand. When this happens, the obvious thing is that you will try to engage in other unimportant activities just to kill time.

However, this doesn't have to be the case, as there is a way to save yourself from the situation. If you are handling strenuous tasks, break them down into smaller tasks. This will help you realize that it is possible to complete the tasks without feeling bored. To ensure that you are excited about the entire process, reward your small efforts. Promise yourself to eat your favorite meal once you are through with the minor tasks. Eventually, you will boost your concentration levels and improve your productivity.

SOCIAL MEDIA

BEARING in mind that you know how addictive social media can be, you should make an effort to avoid the temptation to post your status and reply to your friends' messages. It takes a lot of time to browse through social networks such as Facebook, Twitter, and Instagram. You can bear witness to the fact that once you start responding to texts, your mind will be distracted. You will want to know what your friends are saying about a particular matter at hand. Therefore, it is in your best interest that you postpone your urge to post and reply to messages to a later time when you are free.

STRESS

STRESS WILL DEFINITELY AFFECT your performance at work. Your mind will not be present at whatever you are doing. Rather, your thoughts will easily sink into the difficult moments that you are going through. In extreme cases, you might risk failing to graduate due to a constant decline in your grades.

So, how do you deal with stress? Normally, your stress can be mitigated by engaging in regular exercise. It is a well-known fact that working out can make you feel good about yourself.

Additionally, you should practice meditation. Through meditation, you will boost your level of self-awareness, which will lead
to improved levels of stress management.

Now that you understand the factors that prevent you from
focusing, let's pay close attention to the specific ways you can
sharpen your concentration.

Practicing Pre-Commitment

You can easily boost your concentration by practicing pre-
commitment. Before taking any steps, you should commit yourself ahead of time to whatever you will be doing. In other
words, you should embrace the idea of having a plan for every
task that you will work on throughout the day. Your plan
should detail the amount of time you will spend on each task.
Therefore, whenever you sit down to work on a specific assignment, make sure that nothing diverts your attention until you
complete that specific task.

Enhance Your Focus Muscles

When you hit the gym for the first time, your instructor will
insist on the importance of building your muscles gradually.
You can't wake up one day and decide to lift heavy weights
because this will only harm you. The same thing applies to
your focus muscles. All along, you have been struggling to
concentrate. Therefore, you should start slow and work your
way up gradually.

Challenge yourself with small concentration tasks. This can
be spending 5-10 minutes working on one task without losing

concentration. With time you can challenge yourself to work 30 minutes without being distracted. Remember, after working for about 20-30 minutes, you should take small breaks of about 5 minutes.

Identify Time-Wasters Early Enough

Another effective strategy to bolster your concentration is identifying distractions even before you begin working on an assignment. Create a list of the things that usually waste your time. Afterward, devise a plan of how you will circumvent these time-wasters. For instance, this can include switching off your phone. This will help in clearing your path so that you will focus more on what's important.

Learn to Say "No"

Saying "No" is perhaps one of the most difficult things to do, especially when you are unsure whether it is a prudent decision. It might be difficult to refuse when your friend requests you to go out and have a little fun. However, it is important to note that there is a way of respectfully saying "No" for the right reasons. Bearing in mind that your schedule is fully packed, there is no reason why you should say "Yes" just to please your friend.

SAYING "NO" in such a situation would be helpful because it will prevent you from being distracted by other activities which were not part of your to-do list. Of course, this doesn't mean that you should say no all the time. The idea here is that you should say no when you are certain that you can always o out some other time.

·   ·   ·

DON'T SACRIFICE your time to please others. The bitter truth is that they might never realize that you are giving it your all to ensure that they are pleased. So, stick to your core values and master the art of saying no politely.

Stretch Your Concentration Muscles

In the same way that you need to work gently and stretch well when you hit the gym to strengthen your muscles, you should also think about stretching your concentration muscles. The simplest way to do this is by practicing daily meditation. This doesn't have to be long. By meditating for 10 minutes every day, you can rest assured that you will be more self-aware about what is going on around you. The good news is that you will also find it easy to deal with stress because your mind can focus on what is important in your life.

So FIND an inspiring mantra that you will use during your meditation period. You can choose to meditate either in the morning or in the evening, depending on your schedule. Find a quiet place and recite your mantra for about 10 minutes. Ensure that you focus on how you are saying these words and the thoughts and emotions brought to your mind. When practicing meditation, your focus should not be on the feelings and thoughts that you are experiencing. Rather, you should only be aware of these thoughts and emotions and do nothing about them. This aids your mind in focusing on the mantra regardless of what is going on around you. Do this more often, and your concentration muscles will stretch and become more flexible.

5

IS YOUR SMARTPHONE A TIME WASTER?

Smartphones have indeed revolutionized the way we communicate. With the advent of the internet, people developed a sense that they need always to be connected. Unfortunately, this has led to dwindling productivity among those who use their smartphones every now and then. What's more interesting is that, just a while ago, using your smartphone at work was considered counterproductive. Today, it is the norm. People are no longer afraid that using their smartphones will result in being seen as lazy or distracted. Employers have made things worse by allowing smartphones to be used in places of work. So, you ought to stop and question yourself whether your phone is a time-waster.

You Are Constantly Working

Smartphones provide us with the ability to work on the go. Plenty of applications can be used to bring your work home. Email apps, for example, make it possible to respond to emails without necessarily being at work. While this might sound productive, it's not. Why should you bring work home when you have the whole day to work? Knowing that you do certain activities later at home can simply make you lazy. You can fail to report on a certain project since you will work on it at home. This sounds like procrastination. Therefore, it is imperative to understand how your phone can turn you into a 24-hour working machine.

Constant Notifications

It is quite sad that most of us have turned into slaves of distraction. We have grown to accept that it is normal to be interrupted by texts, emails, and other notifications from the digital spaces that we have signed up with. One of the main reasons it is easy to get distracted by constant notifications from your handset is curiosity. You can't help but wonder what your friends are saying on social media. Also, you might be curious to know what your client said about the project proposal that you offered them.

SUCH DISTRACTIONS HINDER us from being mentally present. You are only physically present, but your mind is somewhere else. To overcome such interruptions, it is advisable to mute these notifications.

A Habit of Multitasking

The constant use of your smartphone will also drive you to develop a habit of multitasking. You will gain the perception that you can complete assignments while at the same time going through Facebook or Twitter notifications. Well, in line with productivity, this is a bad habit.

A Diversion from Productive Communication

Besides luring your mind away from work, your attention will also be diverted away from constructive talks in school. When other students are busy discussing handling their projects and assignments effectively, you might be too busy checking your phone. This prevents you from participating productively in engaging conversations with your schoolmates. This is something that you might have experienced before because your device could make you absent-minded. Instead of contributing to conversations, you find yourself grinning at something that your digital friends have said.

Using Your Phone Productively

The good news is that there are tons of ways to make sure that you use your phone productively. Here are some recommendations about how to use your phone in a way that boosts your productivity.

Separate Yourself from Your Phone

A major issue that turns the phone into a distraction when studying is its physical presence next to you. Most students will often place their devices close to them when studying. Some of us even position these phones in areas where they are easily accessible. For instance, if you are a left-handed person, the chances are that you will have your phone on your left side. This only makes things worse as you will be constantly tempted to check it. What's more, each time you see a notification, it will divert your attention. Therefore, it is wise to store it in a place where you cannot see it.

·   ·   ·

Practice Good Phone Habits

An interesting revelation is that your smartphone use not only affects you but it also affects the people around you. When spending time with family and friends, using your smartphone while talking to them is not the best way of enjoying time together. This is a common habit that is evident in most gatherings with family and friends. People are merely physically present, but they are busy responding to messages on their smartphones.

It is important to practice good phone habits by putting it away each time you communicate with other people. Sure, it might be hard to stay away from your phone for more than 30 minutes. However, it could help in building better connections with people.

Bunch Your Calls

People will often give excuses for the endless use of their phones. Most of them will argue that they have to make important calls, so they deserve to be excused. The reality is that they are only allowing these devices to control them. It is high time that you take control and bunch your calls. Set a time when you can make all these calls at once. This gives you plenty of time to focus on school and less on who's trying to call you.

·   ·   ·

Be Polite and Professional

IF YOU HAVE EVER RECEIVED a phone call from top executives, you must have noticed how polite they are. The first thing they ask is whether it is a good time to communicate. This is being polite, and it shows that the person on the other end of the line values your time. Ideally, this is a habit that you ought to emulate when making calls to other people. Help them understand that time is valuable, and you don't want to waste it talking.

THE CONVENIENCE that the phone provides might blind you to the realization that it is a major distraction to meeting your daily goals. Spending time on the phone is not a bad thing. However, when you are doing it at the expense of your studies, you stand to lose. It is important that you learn how to use your phone to your advantage and not to allow it to act as a time-waster.

6

ENERGY AND TIME MANAGEMENT

Your energy level and motivation are key attributes to successful time management. Just knowing what to do is not enough. Knowledge without proper action will not drive positive results. As Mark Twain was fond of saying "The man who does not read good books has no advantage over the man who can't read them."

YOUR ENERGY, just like your time, is finite. Only it exists in somewhat smaller quantities meaning that it's all too easy to run out and end up completely exhausted. And that's when we start to use our time poorly and not get much done. Many will argue that you have plenty of time. Most of us do have a lot of time; otherwise, how did you manage to stream that entire season of your favorite Netflix or Amazon series? How did you find time for that latest's live stream, or how did you spend two hours today on your social media feeds? And even the busiest of us usually find time for sleep!

. . .

THE POINT here is that time management only works with action and action and motivation are highly dependent on proper energy management. If you don't manage your energy, then you'll find that you're coming back from your daily class schedule completely wiped out.

POOR ENERGY MANAGEMENT is why you end up crashing in front of the TV or staring at your smartphone or computer for hours, and this is one of the key reasons why we don't live life to the fullest! Unfortunately, this creates a negative cycle that makes you even more tired and less energetic because our bodies adapt and become much less efficient. Energy happens at the cellular level; our cells lose mitochondria and become less adept at converting glucose into usable energy. Most people are unaware of this process. People don't routinely think about energy, they don't recognize the importance of energy management, and they certainly are not in the habit of thinking about energy as a finite quantity.

LET'S look at how an example of this plays out every day across our great nation. Somebody somewhere this very moment has bought the latest product on losing weight and getting into shape. They take a look at their current daily activities, and they realize that they're spending a couple of hours in the evening binge-watching Game of Thrones. So, they figure that adding an hour of exercise most evenings shouldn't be a problem, right? So, they come up with an aggressive training program that they think will get the results quickly. Their plan will often include joining a gym, planning on five hours of running/lifting weights a week, and probably a 20 or 30-minute commute to and from the gym for each session. At the same time, they will recognize their eating habits stink, so they will change their diet, typically reducing their carbohydrate intake. With their new plan in hand, they will be filled with enthusiasm, excitement, and expectations for a quick transformation that lays just around the corner. The approach might sound admirable on paper, but in reality, it's completely delusional!

IF YOU'RE CURRENTLY NOT GETTING as much exercise as you think you should be, then it probably means that you're too tired, too low on energy, and too stressed from the daily grind of school or work or both. If you weren't, then you would likely already be more active in the evenings. If you're currently struggling to do anything in the evenings, what makes you think that you're suddenly going to be able to add five hours of intensive activity out of the gate? And all while consuming fewer carbs which are what give us energy in the first place? Do you see the problem here?

TIME IS ONLY useful insofar as you have the energy to make use of it and unfortunately, there's no getting around the fact that you need to rest and recuperate. Your plan may be to spend less time chilling in the evening, but unfortunately, the reality is that most of us can't touch that time. Recharging when you're out of energy is sadly not negotiable!

LOW ENERGY LEVELS leave you with two real options:

- Find ways to increase your energy levels so that you can get more useful hours in the day.
- Prioritize by taking other things out of your routine

to free up both time and energy for exercise or whatever else you want to spend your time on.

Sleeping Habits and Your Energy

Sleep Is Critical

WHAT DO you want to do when you feel really tired and have no energy left to do anything? You go to sleep.

YOUR BODY WILL TELL you quite plainly how important sleep is for energy. Sleep is something of a miracle cure for all kinds of ailments – it improves your memory, focus, attention, mood, and future sleep immensely. Sleeping is far more effective than any beauty treatment, any smart drug, and any supplement. Get the right sleep, and you will be well-positioned to perform on the top of your game the next day – it's that simple.

MOST OF US don't get the quality or the quantity of sleep we need, though, and as such, we find ourselves walking around like zombies. We get cranky, we get easily distracted, we get confused, and generally, we operate like shadows of our true selves. So how do you go about upgrading your sleep and recovering from your low energy levels? Let's take a look at some ways to improve your sleep quality.

TRICKS TO IMPROVE Your Sleep Quality

. . .

TAKE A QUICK CURSORY LOOK ONLINE, and you'll find that there are thousands of different tips and "hacks" that can supposedly give us better sleep. Everyone, it seems, has some tips that can lead to amazing sleep, and indeed there are many good ones out there.

BUT AGAIN, some of them involve a lot of work and very little payoff. So instead, let's focus on the tips that will make a noticeable difference and are relatively easy to implement.

THE GOOD NEWS is that if you're following the tips in this book so far, you should already find yourself sleeping much better. That's because you'll have more energy from more efficient mitochondria – and studies show that this is crucial for sleep. It's again something of a vicious cycle: low energy leads to poor sleep, and poor sleep leads to lower energy!

LIKEWISE, if you're eating healthier, you'll be getting vitamin D, zinc and magnesium, and all kinds of other important nutrients to help your body recover through the night. Finally, if you're reducing your stress, you'll find that this massively has an impact on your ability to sleep as you'll be able to switch off from the stresses of the day much more easily.

LET'S look at some specific actions you can easily take to improve your sleep.

How to Calm Your Mind

.   .   .

BUT WHAT IF you're someone who can't sleep? What if your mind is constantly active and you lie in bed with it racing, unable to switch off?

AN ACTIVE MIND is a problem many students face, and it can severely rob them of their energy levels the next day. You see, when you lie in bed and try to sleep, you might find that it makes you stressed. The fear of not getting to sleep, or the frustration and the expectation, are so great that they cause you to lie awake worrying. Most of us have had that terrible feeling that occurs when we look at the clock and realize we have to be up in just a few hours, and we have not gotten a wink of sleep. An active mind isn't exactly how you sink off to sleep!

TO GET AROUND THIS PROBLEM, we will take a page out of the CBT book (cognitive behavioral therapy). The idea is to change the way you approach and think about sleep. Specifically, you're going to stop pressuring yourself to sleep and to allow instead just yourself to relax. Consider sleep to be a bonus.

TELL yourself that it's fine to relax in bed and enjoy being comfy – because it is. That's good for you too. You can't force yourself to sleep, so don't try. Just lie there and enjoy not having to do anything, enjoy not having to be anywhere, and enjoy the feeling of closing your eyes and listening to your breathing.

WHAT YOU'LL FIND, quite ironically, is that as soon as you start taking this approach, you drift right off!

.   .   .

SHOULD YOU POWER NAP?

EVEN IF YOU have the best plans and intentions in the world, there will be moments when you don't get the best sleep and all of your sleeping tactics fail you. What do you do in those situations? One smart strategy is to give it another shot later.

POWER NAPPING CAN HELP you get some rest, and several studies have shown that it can improve your productivity, mood, and other aspects of your life.

So, how do you take a proper nap? The key is to time it perfectly, aiming for a minimum of twenty minutes and a maximum of ninety minutes, not more and not less. The way our bodies cycle through different stages of sleep (the body likes rhythms!) necessitates the employment of these time bands. You will go through one entire sleep cycle in 90 minutes, going from the lightest stage of sleep to SWS (slow wave sleep) to REM (rapid eye movement) (rapid eye movements). You'll start to come around as soon as you wake up. You can also sleep for twenty minutes and then wake up before entering the deeper stages of sleep to avoid sleep inertia. If we have an option, ninety minutes is a better way to improve our performance.

THE POWER SLEEP works like this: A power nap takes use of the benefits of the first two stages of your sleep cycle, which recur throughout a typical night's sleep. As electrical brain activity, eye and jaw-muscle action, and respiration slow down during the first sleep stage, you drop deeper into sleep. The second stage is light but peaceful sleep in which the body prepares for the deep and dreamless "slow-wave sleep," or SWS, that happens in stages three and four by reducing temperature and relaxing muscles even more. REM is the fifth stage, which occurs when dreaming gets more intense.

EVERY NINETY TO one hundred and twenty minutes, the five sleep stages resume their cycle. The first stage can last up to ten minutes, and the second stage can take up to twenty minutes. In stage two, we experience unique electrical signals in the nervous system that establish the connection between neurons involved in muscle memory, making the twenty-minute nap essential for the hard-working student wanting to recoup from a few days of missing sleep.

TAKE a Hot Bath or Shower Before Bed

ONE OF THE most effective strategies to aid deeper sleep is to take a shower. Taking a hot shower right before bed will not only relax your muscles, but it will also cause your body to create growth hormones and melatonin, putting you to sleep.

ALLOW yourself a half-hour of rest before going to bed.

THIS IS the one life hack that absolutely everyone should follow these days. Whatever else is going on in your life, set aside half an hour before bedtime to unwind and read a book. Turn off your phone and read with only a dim lamp on. Treat this time as "wind-down" time by not watching TV, checking social

media, or having meaningful conversations with your
roommate.

AS A RESULT OF THIS PROCESS, your mind will begin to relax and
shed the pressures of the day, allowing you to feel more
comfortable. In addition, less screen time means your brain
will be able to produce more melatonin. When you gaze at a
computer or television screen, your brain interprets the light's
wavelength as sunlight. As a result, your brain behaves as if it's
daytime, flooding your body with cortisol and keeping you
from sleeping. And this is why it's critical to ensure that your
room has very little light.

THE ADVANTAGES of having a half-hour to oneself to relax go far
beyond improved sleep. Your life as a student is hectic, and you
rarely have free time. It's common to feel as if you've reached
your limit. Beginning to take time off to unwind will make
school and life seem much more manageable.

GET Into a Routine

SOMETHING important to understand about the human body is
that it works to rhythms. Your body likes routine because this
allows it to learn natural rhythms – highs and lows that will
stay consistent, ensuring you start winding down biologically at
the right moment.

ROUTINES CAN MAKE a big difference in your ability to doze off,
and it will also allow you to control the amount of sleep you're

getting more closely. As you likely know, eight hours is a good ball-park figure to aim for if you can. Very few people can function properly in less than six hours of sleep a night.

PERFECT YOUR ENVIRONMENT

THESE ARE THE "EASY TIPS" that pretty much everyone already knows about sleeping – but they're important, and so they're still very much worth going over. Your environment is another key to optimal sleep.

- Since most dorms can be quite loud, use a sleep machine or fan to create white noise and block out as much noise as possible.
- Get your dorm room or apartment as pitch black as possible.
- Keep your room as clean as possible.
- Invest in a mattress topper to make your bed comfortable.

OBVIOUSLY, it's also very important to wear comfortable sleepwear, invest in a comfortable bed if you are off campus (one of the best purchases you will ever make), and keep your room at the right temperature. The ideal temperature is for your room to be cool, which is how we are evolutionarily designed to sleep.

· · ·

IN THE PREVIOUS SECTION, we looked at how to get off to sleep and ensure we sleep well. That's one part of the story but what comes next is waking up the next day. How do you ensure you can spring out of bed and get lots done?

Your Morning Schedule and Your Energy

How to Wake Up Full of Energy

NOW THAT YOU know how to get to sleep, the next question is how you can wake up energized. Waking up is the key piece of the puzzle that most people overlook when it comes to sleeping well – but having a good night's sleep does not necessarily mean you'll be able to wake up easily too!

TOO MANY OF us wake up feeling groggy, sluggish, and tired, and as a result, we waste the first half of the day. Some of us will even feel sick in the morning or have bad headaches.

IF YOU FALL into this latter category, then, of course, this is not normal, should not be considered "okay," and is something you should discuss with your doctor. A few common culprits for feeling sick, having headaches, or feeling "drained" in the morning include:

DEHYDRATION – Try drinking a large glass of water before bed, and you won't wake up with a dry throat or a headache.

. . .

LOW BLOOD SUGAR – When you go to sleep, you are essentially fasting for 8 hours straight without food. As a result, you can feel sick when you wake up. Some theorists even believe that this is why we have grown to eat dessert as the last meal of the day! Some people recommend having a teaspoon of honey before bed to provide a steady flow of sugar (sucrose and fructose) throughout the night.

MOLD – If you have mold in your room this can leave you feeling ill owing to the mycotoxins that it releases. Some signs of mold include a musky smell and damp air. If you notice these things, it can be worth having campus maintenance or a remediation company check things out – even if you can't see mold it can sometimes be building up underneath the floorboards or behind the paint in your rooms!

ALLERGIES – If you're waking up hoarse with a headache, then allergies are a common cause. Even if you don't think you have any allergies, remember that they can come on at any point during your lifetime, and as such, you may have developed hay fever or similar allergen. Allergies are especially common if you go to school out of state as you experience a completely new set of allergens.

SLEEP APNEA – Sleep apnea is a condition that causes you to wake up for brief spells during the night because you've stopped breathing. In some cases, this is due to a blocked passage (obstructive apnea), but in others, it may have no cause (primary apnea). The best way to diagnose this is to see a doctor. Bring a video of yourself sleeping, ask a friend to watch you, your doctor will potentially have you visit a sleep clinic.

Either way, you might be prescribed a CPAP (continuous positive airway pressure) device to prevent the problem. If you are snoring, this may be a sign of sleep apnea, be sure to discuss this situation with your doctor.

IF YOU ADDRESS ALL these factors, you should find you start feeling much fresher and more energetic in the morning.

SOMETHING else that can help is to look into getting a "daylight lamp." These lamps emit a light wave very similar to the sun and will gradually get brighter in the morning. Daylight lamps can help to gradually nudge you out of deep sleep rather than waking you in the deepest stages of sleep. At the same time, these lamps can help to combat mild cases of "SAD" (seasonal affective disorder), which is a condition that leaves people feeling tired, lethargic, and even potentially depressed during the darker winter months. It can also help put your biological clock more in sync with your routine. In general, it's a very useful tool for waking up more gradually and naturally – it's certainly much better than being startled out of your sleep by a blaring alarm clock.

AND ANOTHER TRICK you can use that's slightly controversial for waking up in the morning is to use your phone. Many people will tell you not to use your phone in the morning to get up, but if you're someone who struggles to wake in the morning, it can be useful. The idea here is to set yourself up to receive something you're looking forward to in the morning – subscribe to some good YouTube channels, for instance, or join a Facebook community on a subject you're interested. Interesting content will serve as a motivation to get up first thing in the morning to grab your phone. If you can motivate yourself to do just that little bit and to start reading, you'll find that you gradually come around.

THERE'S AN APP FOR THAT – You might also consider using an app that offers sleep tracking. A great example of this would be Sleep Cycle and Pillow. These apps have a great feature that will wake you up from a light sleep by watching your movement during the night. You set the alarm – say for 7 am – and it waits for a moment near then when you're in light sleep rather than deep sleep. It might go off at 6.30 am, for instance, or 6.45 am but never after 7 am. This means you're now waking up out of light sleep instead of a heavy sleep, which helps prevent "sleep inertia." In theory, you should be much more awake.

SLEEP TRACKERS – can be great for improving energy in other ways too. Some have a constant heart rate monitor, which allows you to measure your heart rate throughout the night. Sleep trackers will give you a much more accurate measure of your sleep as well as your calories burned, and that in turn will allow you to run experiments to see which sleeping strategies are the most effective for helping you get proper rest.

WHAT TO DO FIRST?

SO, now you're out of bed, what do you do first? A healthy breakfast is a great start to your day and a coffee if you're so inclined (though in the long term, caffeine does more harm than good to energy levels).

· · ·

USING THE TIPS ABOVE, you should be feeling fairly awake, but even with the best routines in the world, you'll still potentially feel a little groggy in the morning sometimes and need a bit of help waking up.

ONE THING that can help you to wake up then is to take a cold shower. A cold shower will not only shock you into wakefulness; it will trigger the release of norepinephrine and dopamine thus making you more alert and even speed up your metabolism to burn more fat. As a way to wake up, this beats a cup of coffee any day!

NEXT, you'll probably have to head off to class. If you are off-campus in a big city, then your commute is one of the very worst things for many when it comes to stress and energy. Not only is it stressful sitting in traffic or on a busy train, but it's also a waste of energy. What's more, if you walk on busy streets in the morning, your body will view this as the equivalent of being repeatedly surprised by hundreds of people. Did you know that "things moving toward us" is a universal fear that we all share? Fear and stress can drastically raise your heart rate and make you feel rather exhausted when you get into the classroom.

WHAT'S THE SOLUTION? Live on or very close to campus. Of course, you should look for a less stressful commute if possible, but at the very least, keep your commute time in mind when thinking about your energy and stress levels and be mindful to stay calm and relaxed.

· · ·

IF YOU ARE NOT RUNNING off to class, when starting your day, remember that you're not performing at your absolute optimum when you first get up. A good type of work, to begin with, is something that you can do relatively mindlessly.

WHEN WE FEEL low on energy, exercise can often feel like the last thing we want to do. However, exercising is one of the most powerful ways to boost energy levels in both the very short term and the much longer term.

Exercise and Your Energy

Let's take a look at how exercise improves your energy.

SHORT TERM

IN THE SHORT TERM, exercise can give you a great energy boost which is why it's a good way to start your day. One reason exercising is so good for you in the short term is that it encourages healthy circulation. Exercise gets your heart beating which sends more blood to your muscles and your brain. That means more oxygen and more nutrients which is essentially like getting an injection of rocket fuel!

EXERCISE ALSO STIMULATES the release of lots of very positive hormones and neurotransmitters. If you've heard of the "runners-high," then you should know that jogging can stimulate the release of endorphins and serotonin. The result is that you feel very positive, very happy and of course very high in energy.

. . .

As a bonus, exercise is also one of the most potent ways to boost the therapeutic nature of your sleep (we saved this one!). When you work out during the day, you will burn more energy, which means you will be more likely to doze off at night, especially if you got lots of fresh air by working out outside.

Long Term

But the long-term benefits of exercise are much more profound. For starters, exercise will help you to burn calories and lose weight. Proper weight management means you'll be carrying less weight around with you and will feel lighter, nimbler, and far more energetic as a result.

On top of this, exercise will also help to improve your fitness. Improved fitness levels result in a stronger heart and a better VO_2 max. VO_2 refers to your body's ability to bring in oxygen and to utilize it for energy in a short space of time. A high VO_2 max means that you can run long distances without panting or feeling out of breath. Exercise also just so happens to be the perfect antidote to all that sitting in class.

And if you can run a long distance without feeling out of breath, imagine how much easier that walk to class or that hike up to the grocery store will be!

Exercise also builds muscle, and believe it or not, that can also help you feel more energetic. The main reason for this is that it makes various activities less strenuous and tiring. If you've built strong muscles, then you'll find lifting things much easier, walking much easier, and pretty much everything else much easier too!

BETTER YET, exercise can also boost your mitochondrial count. Your mitochondria are the energy centers of your cells that help you utilize ATP and power yourself through your day.

EXERCISE INCREASES the quantity and efficiency of mitochondria and especially when you use HIIT. HIIT stands for "High-Intensity Interval Training" and is a type of exercise that involves brief bursts of exertion lasting a couple of minutes, followed by longer bursts of active recovery.

So, while some exercise programs might have you running on a treadmill for ten minutes at fifty percent of your maximum capacity, a HIIT workout would involve sprinting on a treadmill for thirty seconds to two minutes. Power walking for three or four minutes and then sprinting for another thirty seconds two minutes for usually six to eight cycles. This type of exercise is more efficient in a shorter period and is generally a great way to give yourself a boost mentally and physically.

HOW TO TRAIN

USING HIIT is a good idea to get the most energy benefit in the shortest time. It would be best to combine this with some weight lifting to benefit from more physical strength (and weightlifting is very good for weight loss and improving your metabolism). I recommend three days of HITT with two days of weight training.   You Might schedule HIIT on Monday, Wednesday, and Friday, with weight training on Tuesday, Thursdays. Some students prefer three days of weights and two days of HIIT; both schedules are effective.

WHAT'S ALSO important is to avoid overdoing your training. Overdoing it is the big mistake that many people make when taking on any new workout routine, and it can end up being almost as bad as not exercising at all.

IF YOU LIFT weights until you are sore, for instance, then bear in mind that this now means you're going to be sore for the rest of that day and probably for the next two days. What's the point of being at your physical best if you hurt every time you move? Likewise, if you run too far and too fast, you'll end up feeling too weak and low on energy for the following days and nights. Continue this over-exertion too long, and it can eventually lead to "overtraining," which leaves you feeling tired, listless, and upset.

SOMETHING TO PAY attention to here is your heart rate variance. Heart rate variance shows you how well recovered you are after an interval and workout. Please make sure you train to the point where it's still fun, push yourself but not too hard, and listen to what your body is telling you.

REMEMBER - It is important that you visit a doctor before starting any diet or exercise training program.

Your Diet and Your Energy

Diet is one of the most significant contributors to low energy, particularly in general and students.

WE WOULD HAVE EATEN a diet that gave us a lot of energy and allowed us to chase down prey and perform at our best in general back in the caveman days. It is not by chance that the food accessible to us provided us with so much energy and that our bodies evolved as they did due to that diet. To put it another way, we evolved over thousands of years to flourish on what was available to us.

MANY OF US are now surviving on a diet devoid of all of that goodness (or at least barely any). Consult your doctor before beginning any diet, supplement, or fitness program to ensure that you do so safely.

LOW-DENSITY, Low-Carbohydrate Diets

IF YOU'RE like most people, you'll come home after class and pop a pizza in the microwave, grab something from the university vending machines, or get a cappuccino and croissant.

LET'S have a look at what you receive as a result of this. Well, you do receive a lot of calories in terms of energy. A typical store-bought scone contains around 600 calories. Then there's the vending machine chips, which will add another 200 calories to your diet, plus your drink and dessert, which will add even more calories.

YOU'VE MOST likely consumed over 1,000 calories by the end, which is around half of most people's daily calorie intake. A poor diet causes us to gain weight, and lugging that additional weight about with you is an unavoidable source of exhaustion.

IT'S ALSO NOT a good idea to cram so much food into your body at once. You now have a large amount of food to process, including low-quality protein, which will slowly pass through your digestive system, depleting your energy for other processes.

IN ADDITION, the calories you just consumed were "simple carbs." The scone, chips, dessert, and drink are all simple sweets that rapidly spike the bloodstream. That's before you factor in all of the additional sugar. Suddenly bombarding your body with that much raw energy may appear to be beneficial to your energy, but nothing could be farther from the truth. Instead, you're boosting your blood sugar, which causes an insulin spike, resulting in a high. Insulin metabolizes sugar and eliminates it from your bloodstream, but it is merely stored as fat because you aren't utilizing it rapidly enough (a process called lipogenesis). And guess how you'll feel once it's finished? Exhausted! And you're hit by a wave of exhaustion (which, by the way, is when most of us snack on more sugar).

WORSE YET, all those calories and simple carbohydrates have done you no good. Why? The scone is made entirely of flour and sugar, and the chips have little nutritional value. So, every day, all you're doing is stuffing your body with low-quality, large-quantity food to process. Is it any surprise that you're exhausted?

Supplements That Provide Energy

I could tell you to get rid of it right now. Stop eating that crap and reintroduce a healthy diet. However, it would be ineffective.

I'm not sure how I can be confident of that. Because you already knew your diet wasn't particularly healthy. You already know how much better home-cooked fresh ingredients are.

What is the issue? You don't have the time, energy, or money to change your eating habits. It's worth noting that energy is an issue here: it's a bit of a vicious circle, isn't it?

So, to jumpstart your self-improvement and drive towards more energy, why don't we start with a supplement stack. The following items can be taken with your meals to boost your energy levels significantly:

Vitamin D is excellent for two things: improving your sleep and helping you to produce more testosterone. The vast majority of us are deficient, so take this in the morning, and you'll start feeling a lot better.

. . .

IRON AND VITAMIN B12 are required to give us our healthy red blood cells. In case you forgot, red blood cells are the oxygen-carrying portion of our blood which our body uses to burn fat and fuel all kinds of processes in our body.

OMEGA 3 FATTY Acid is an essential fatty acid that the body uses to create cell walls. Increasing your cell membrane permeability is very important. Why? Because it helps the cells communicate with one another, it allows neurotransmitters to pass more easily between brain cells.

CREATINE IS a supplement used by athletes. Its job is to take the broken-down form of ATP (adenosine triphosphate) and recombine it for extra use in the body. What does this mean? Well, ATP is the main energy currency of all life. It comes from glucose and releases energy when the bonds connecting three molecules break apart. This results in ADP (adenosine diphosphate) and AMP (adenosine monophosphate) – a two for one. Normally, that's all the use you can get out of it, but you can reuse the energy by re-bonding the ADP and AMP back together with creatine.

THE BODY PRODUCES CREATINE NATURALLY, but you can get a little more if you take it in supplement form. In real terms, this means a few extra seconds of exertion when lifting weights or running a marathon – and it means better mental energy for performing your school work and fighting the daily stresses of college life.

· · ·

LUTEIN IS GENERALLY THOUGHT of as a supplement for the eyes to help prevent macular degeneration. Recent studies suggest it could also enhance the performance of the mitochondria – the energy factories that live inside each of our cells. When given to mice, they would voluntarily run miles further each week on their treadmills – pointing to increased energy and performance.

GARLIC EXTRACT IS A VASODILATOR. Vasodilator means that it can widen the blood vessels to allow more blood and oxygen to get around – to the brain and muscles, for instance - thus fueling you with more energy.

VITAMIN B6 IS USED to help us extract energy from carbohydrates. At the same time, B6 helps with the creations of neurotransmitters which helps it to boost cognitive performance. Low levels of B6 have been shown to result in a lack of energy and focus and even shrinking brain tissue and Alzheimer's.

COENZYME Q10 IS another substance that athletes are very interested in and which can considerably increase the efficiency of the mitochondria for enhanced fat burning and energy production.

THE PERFECT DIET

NOW THAT'S a lot of different supplements to be taking. It's quite a long shopping list, and it would get pretty expensive.

Here's the thing, though: you needn't be taking any of these supplements. Not if your diet is correct.

ALL OF THESE things can be found in your diet if you know where to look. CoQ10 and creatine are in red meats, vitamins and minerals are in all our fruits and vegetables, omega three fatty acids is in fish, lutein is in eggs.

IF YOU MAKE sure that everything you're eating is fresh and nutritious, then you'll be providing your body with all the energy it needs. You'll be able to absorb it better, and you'll be getting it in the right ratios and quantities. Meanwhile, other substances found in your diet can help to boost your energy levels as well: zinc, magnesium, vitamin C, PQQ, l-carnitine, l-theanine, and resveratrol are just a few. Eating a healthy diet is like having an incredibly expensive athlete's supplement stack! Only better.

MEANWHILE, you should try to avoid "simple" carbs. That's anything that tastes sweet (like cake) and anything white (like pasta or rice). Instead, start eating brown rice, and pasta, vegetables, spinach and have that in the place of your chips (as a rule, try to avoid processed, human-made carbs). Proper nutrition will allow the body to release energy much more slowly and provide you with a steady supply throughout the day. Don't be afraid of fat either – it contains more calories (9 per gram versus 4), but it's slow release too. Try to eat smaller portions, more often and don't over-stuff yourself.

·   ·   ·

How do you go about cooking these nutritious, fresh meals when you lack time and energy? A good plan is to prepare your meals at the start of the week. Cook up a few pots of food you can dip into throughout the week and keep what you don't eat in the freezer or plastic containers. If you purchased your universities meal plan, you generally could save time by cutting out the shopping and preparation time. Most universities now provide healthy and well-balanced meal options if you have the willpower to skip the dessert bar! A few students report they hate cooking because their roommates expect them to prepare food for them. If you live on campus in a dorm, a meal plan is likely your best choice. Most universities' meal plans include dollars to eat at your on-campus Chick-Fil-A, Starbucks, Panera, or national food chain of choice.

On-Going Too Far

We eat too many processed carbs. And if we ate less of those carbs, we'd feel much better. At the same time, though, we still need carbs. They're still an important food group in our diet, and if we get the right kind in the right quantities, they boost testosterone production and aid with our general levels of energy and well-being. Restrict carbs too much, and you'll feel tired. The occasional bit of brown pasta with your bolognese won't kill you. Many old-school bodybuilders eat nothing but rice and steamed chicken when training for competition.

Likewise, while natural, unprocessed foods are healthier than cake, pie, and chips, you don't need to eat only the things you would find in caveman days. A lot of serious Paleo dieters will tell you not to eat bread, wheat, or cheese. And they will never break their diet to have a bowl of pasta.

BUT HERE'S THE THING: most of the top-performing athletes in the world have performed just fine on bread. Some of the smartest thinkers in the world drank lots of tea and ate lots of chocolate.

POINT BEING? You can perform just fine eating a relatively "normal" diet. And, our lifestyle places different demands on our body these days anyway; it's only natural our diet should adjust. In other words, don't waste your energy thinking you can only eat specific foods. Start with your current diet but make it a little healthier by cutting back on the simple carbs and by injecting more nutrients. As you feel the results, you will find your body will crave the junk less, and before you know it, your diet will be quite healthy. Some emerging research indicates gluten-free diets may have a significant impact on long-term positive brain function. As diet science constantly evolves, it makes sense to approach your nutrition and diet with a grain of salt and practice moderation in your approaches. Pay attention to how your body responds to your diet and adjust accordingly. Make sure to get an annual physical that includes blood work, as it is essential to consult your physician before making changes to your diet, taking supplements, or starting an exercise program.

Habits and Lifestyle Impact Your Energy

Once you've upgraded your diet, you'll find that you immediately start feeling more energetic. Diet is a critical part of the battle. But to improve your energy, you need to look at the bigger picture. No part of our health exists in a vacuum, and even the best diet in the world can't stand up to the wrong lifestyle or the wrong routine.

You're probably doing a bunch of things right now that are completely ruining your energy levels. If you can find these energy black holes, then you'll be able to save yourself large packets of energy to use in other, more constructive ways throughout the day.

Alcohol and Your Energy

Here comes the bad news alcohol is very bad for your energy levels. As in, it's down-right awful.

In the short term, alcohol is terrible for your energy and can leave you completely exhausted. Alcohol is a depressant, which means that it works to inhibit the firing of neurons in your brain, slowing down your thinking and making you sleepy. Alcohol, like a sleeping pill or anxiolytic, works the opposite of a stimulant. And because it causes whole areas of the brain to stop working, it can rob you of your higher-order brain function too.

If you plan to be productive, think twice about picking up that beer or glass of wine. Drinking alcohol also has longer-term effects on your energy levels and general health. Of course, alcohol also contributes to weight gain at seven calories per gram. It can cause headaches the next day, and it significantly impairs the quality of your sleep. Try wearing a heart rate monitor when you drink alcohol, and you'll see it sends it sky-high, which isn't exactly conducive to a restful night! Although alcohol is a depressant, it amps up the body as it tries to purge what is essentially a toxin from your system.

IF YOU'RE DRINKING ALCOHOL, try to have your last glass a few hours before bed. And try eating a banana and honey sandwich as a hangover cure. It can work wonders as the banana and honey will line the stomach, replenish your energy stores, fix your electrolytes and break down acetaldehyde – a toxic substance responsible for a lot of the negative effects associated with a hangover.

WATER

So, if you shouldn't be drinking alcohol, what you should be drinking is water.

WATER IS crucial to your energy levels as it's what the body uses for pretty much every crucial function. You've probably read stats telling you that your body is seventy percent water or thereabout, and it's true – you are mostly water.

TOO BAD THEN THAT the majority of the US population are chronically dehydrated! Dehydration leads to headaches, cramps, dry throats, and of course – tiredness.

. . .

How MUCH WATER should you be drinking? A good guide is to try and consume at least seven to ten glasses a day. Try this, and you should find that you start feeling energized. And remember, dehydration kills your cognitive function by up to 30%.

SITTING TOO Much

AS A STUDENT, the simple fact of the matter is that you probably sit far too much. You are sitting in class, sitting in the library, sitting in your dorm, etc.

SITTING IS bad for us for all kinds of reasons. The main one, though, is that it's terrible for our hearts – the longer you spend sitting during the day, the more health issues you are likely to develop over the longer term.

STRESS MANAGEMENT

SITTING for long durations is bad, but stress is potentially more destructive, which many of us experience on campus and on the job. If you are very stressed at school, you should not underestimate just what a severe impact this can have on your health, mood, and energy levels.

THE IDEA of stress is to increase our awareness, physical strength, and ability to think quickly. Thus, when we are stressed, our bodies respond by releasing dopamine, norepinephrine, and other "fight or flight" hormones. The chemical releases in your body increase your heart rate, direct more blood flow to the muscles and the brain, and heighten our awareness. At the same time, we might start trembling, our immune and digestive systems become suppressed, and we'll feel anxious and jittery.

ALL THESE EFFECTS are designed to help us in a fight or flight situation. In other words, they are meant to come on fast and be over quickly. If we saw a predator or prey, if we fought with someone, or if we saw a fire – then this would be exactly how the fight or flight system would work and, it would probably help us stay alive.

TODAY THOUGH, stress is not acute – it is chronic. Our modern sources of stress include exams, projects, papers, angry bosses, poor finances, strained relationships, and looming deadlines; all these things have no finite end or no imminent end at least. In other words, our body is constantly in this state of arousal, and as such, our immune system is constantly suppressed, leaving us susceptible to illness. Likewise, our digestion is also robbing us of the nutrients we should be getting from our food.

AND EVENTUALLY, the brain will run low on those fight or flight hormones. At this point, your sympathetic nervous system burns out, and you reach a point known as adrenal fatigue. You will then find yourself robbed of the neurotransmitters that normally help you get up in the morning and focus on the task at hand. And without these neurotransmitters, you will feel demotivated, low on energy, and listless – low levels of neuro-transmitters lead to depression.

· · ·

So, if you're getting to that point where you have no energy in the morning and where it's all just starting to feel a little bit too hard to carry on – you're probably experiencing adrenal fatigue as a result of stress.

IF YOU ARE in that situation, you should change some aspect of your lifestyle or routine. While it might not be easy to change your major or transfer schools, take time out of a relationship, or speak to a counselor – you must take positive actions. Ultimately, your health and your quality of life are what you should be putting first - above all else.

USING ALL the advice we've covered so far in this book, you should now be reaching the point where you are well prepared to manage your time, schedule, and energy. Even with this knowledge, though, it's important to realize that you still aren't completely in charge of everything, and you're still in some ways restricted by higher forces.

SPECIFICALLY, your energy will rise and fall with your body's natural rhythms. Your energy levels ebb and flow like waves, and at some points, you will be high in energy, and at other points, you will be low in energy. Energy levels are set partly by your internal body clock (internal pacemaker) and partly by external cues (external zeitgebers) such as social cues, eating habits, and light.

WHEN YOU WAKE UP, your body is flooded with cortisol, which helps you start shifting into first gear. Your energy then remains fairly steady until lunch, when you replenish your glucose stores and then again at 4 pm at which point you will reach a low point in your natural energy cycle. 4 pm is when many of us start feeling sleepy and wanting to curl up on the couch. We also feel tired after eating food while we're digesting, so if you eat a meal at 3.30pm, you may as well write 4 pm off completely.

Your energy will improve after 4 pm but will slowly tail off until bedtime. There will be another slump, peak, and slump following dinner.

Structuring Your Day for Optimum Productivity

Simply knowing that these ebbs and flows exist and knowing when you're going to perform your best can help a great deal with your ability to stay productive and get the most out of yourself.

Another tip is to avoid having big plans after dinner. If you have anything productive to do, then do it before you eat. The minute you eat dinner and sit on the couch, your energy will be in decline, and your ability to be productive will decline significantly.

Ebbs and flows apply on a larger scale as well. Specifically, you will find that you also have months where energy is high and months where you struggle. This ebb and flow can impact your exercise – you can have months of being highly disciplined and training well and then have months of low energy or a feeling you have plateaued. Don't punish yourself when this happens. Go with your body's natural inclination and try to plan tasks for the points in time when you are most likely to focus on and complete them.

INDIVIDUAL DIFFERENCES and How to Control Your Cycles

WE'VE LOOKED at the times you're most likely to be productive or sleepy during the day, and for most people, this will ring true. However, keep in mind that everyone is different. Some people are night owls and are more productive later at night, while other people are early birds and will tend to get their best work done first thing in the morning when the rest of us are still groggy and experiencing sleep inertia. Pay attention to your energy levels throughout the day, learn your cycles, and work to optimize your schedule continually within those natural rhythms.

AT THE SAME TIME, remember that you can control your rhythms to help your energy cycles sync up with what you're doing at any given time. The daylight lamp we mentioned earlier is one, and another is to time when you eat carefully. Not only can changing your eating schedule help you move that after-dinner slump, but it also actually affects your body clock. Eat dinner later, and you'll find it a little easier to sleep later. Daytime naps can also help with this.

THROUGHOUT THIS BOOK, we've covered a lot of different points, and right now your mind might be swimming with ideas for how to get more energy and how to change your routine for the better.

To help you cement all these ideas then, let's quickly recap on some of the tools and strategies you can now be using to get more energy:

Start eating more healthily
- Avoid processed foods
- Avoid simple carbohydrates
- Eat nutrient-dense foods
- Eat smaller meals, more regularly
- Eat complex carbs that release energy more slowly
- Don't get too carried away with fad diets
- Prepare meals in advance
- Supplement if necessary

Exercise more
- Use HIIT training to increase mitochondria
- Don't overtrain

Manage your sleep
- Have half an hour to relax in the evenings
- Take a hot shower before bed

Wake up slowly
- Use a sleep tracker
- Tempt yourself out of bed with something interesting
- Take a cold shower!

. . .

PLAN YOUR DAY TO **coincide with your natural energy highs and lows**
- Do productive things first
- Time meals to adjust your body clock

Learn what works for you!

All of this might sound like quite a lot and especially if you're feeling low on energy. If you're exhausted right now, then can you be bothered to take up a new exercise program? Can you find the energy to bike to class? How will you ever find the time to change your whole routine? Find time to cook these fresh, healthy meals?

ALL THESE STRATEGIES might sound like a lot, and it might sound daunting, but that's why it can pay to keep in mind the Japanese principle of Kaizen. Kaizen means making small, incremental changes that all add up to something big and profound. It is like the Magic Penny doubling each day to create millions.

A SMALL STEP, like swapping your morning donut and coffee for a smoothie and experiencing how much more energy you get from this small change, will build momentum. It's a very small change, but it will make a huge difference, and you will find it very motivating.

IF YOU CAN'T COMMIT to half an hour of winding down in the evening, try making it ten minutes. If you can't commit to twenty minutes of meditation, do five minutes.

AND IF WORKING out five days a week is too daunting, commit to half an hour twice a week to begin. You get the idea.

THIS STRATEGY of small incremental changes is the exact game plan coach Pat Riley used with the Los Angeles Lakers to win the NBA Championship in the 1987-1988 season. During the previous season, the team had self-destructed during the Western Conference Finals, losing to Houston. Coach Riley spent the summer uncovering what went wrong, where they would need to improve their game to win the championship. Coach Riley and his staff identified five areas that each player on the team needed to improve.

DURING TRAINING CAMP for the next season, the coach challenged each player to improve one percent above the career-best in each of five areas. One percent doesn't seem like much, but if you take a dozen players on the team and each improves one percent in five areas, the team gains a whopping 60% improvement in overall performance.

BECAUSE THE PLAYERS saw one percent as very achievable, they could focus their efforts on small, realistic actions to improve. The results were amazing, with most players improving double digits, and one player improved an amazing 50 percent. The individual improvements translated to 67 team wins and an NBA Championship. The following season the team would repeat as champions, becoming the first team in nineteen years to win back-to-back titles.

. . .

SMALL, focused changes can go a long way on your road to success. And whether your goal is to win an NBA Championship, land that perfect job, or launch your own business, ultimately applying small changes and watching them compound over time will lead to massive success. And it all starts with just one small change!

7

CREATING BALANCE IN YOUR LIFE

Social life, hobbies, sports, friends, personal growth, learning independence, and other aspects of school life are all vital, and you must make use of all of them. However, there must be a balance struck. Too much of anything might detract from the broader strategic purpose of time management.

USE the tips and strategies outlined in this chapter to help improve and re-balance your life.

Working While in School

One of the hardest realities of the present educational system for many students is working part-time or even full-time. Every student's financial situation is unique, and only a small percentage of students have parents who have an infinite amount of income. Many young adults need to work to make ends meet, while others prefer to work to lessen their reliance on financial help or scholarships. So, how can you strike a balance between your career and your other obligations?

THE MOST IMPORTANT thing to remember is to communicate your daily class schedule. Make sure your boss is aware of your class schedule and speak with him or her about your time requirements. Many employers understand the struggles of working students. To have a successful coexistence with your career and your schooling, you must communicate.

MANY FAMILY-OWNED businesses are more accepting of students and are eager to work with full-time students as employees.

LOOK into getting a job on campus. Look for employment that fits into your schedule on bulletin boards, websites, the career office, and so on, or contact the human resources department and inquire about open positions. The majority of colleges will give you work in your subject of study. Working on campus eliminates commute time to off-campus employment and reduces the burden of juggling classes and work.

IN ANY PARTICULAR SEMESTER, don't try to take on too many hours. According to studies, students who work more than 15 hours at a part-time job while taking a full course load experience higher stress and are more likely to drop out of school due to that stress. While it's critical to have enough money to cover bills, it's also critical to focus on your academics.

. . .

MAKE the most of your free time. Review your notecards when you take a break, and read a chapter while eating a sandwich at your lunch or supper break. Discuss with your boss the possibility of studying on the job during lulls. If you work in a retail business, for example, see if your manager will let you study in between customers. When you make the most of your time, your chances of balancing work and academics improve dramatically.

WORKING while in college provides the student with more benefits than just the opportunity to earn money. Students can collaborate with teachers and administrators on campus, who can often function as mentors. Additionally, students can frequently find occupations related to their academic studies (lab work, research, etc.). Moreover, campus employment frequently allows students to explore a variety of career alternatives. At the very least, prospective employers value the fact that students worked during their undergraduate years.

IF YOU HAVE A JOB, don't be scared to tell your teachers. Most teachers have learned to ignore students who make bad reasons for not completing their tasks on time, but that doesn't mean they won't make an exception when necessary.

WORKING while in college is beneficial, but it is not for everyone. Working, like the rest of one's college life, should be viewed in context. Working should be a supplement to a student's academic endeavors rather than a detriment. Try it out; if it doesn't work or you run into academic issues, speak with your academic dean. Immediately!

. . .

IF WORKING GETS TOO MUCH, consider other routes for earning cash or modify your budget. You should NEVER let work hold you back from achieving your dream of a college education. There are many resources available. Take advantage of them! Use them! Go to the financial aid office and discuss your situation with a counselor there. You might be surprised by the options available.

CONSIDER some of these other tips:

- Get a work-study job if you are eligible. The Federal Work-Study Program offers jobs to eligible Federal financial aid recipients. If you receive Federal financial aid, your award letters will identify whether you are eligible for work-study and the number of hours you will be allowed to work.
- If you are eligible, you can go to your financial aid office and apply for available work-study jobs. These jobs can either be on campus or off-campus and are usually at a non-profit organization or public agency. These organizations generally let students work very flexible hours.
- Get a job that includes tips. Jobs with wages plus tips often pay the best. So, if you are looking to earn more money while in college, consider being a waiter, waitress or bartender at a local restaurant. Just keep in mind that these job hours may not be as flexible as a job on campus or a work-study job.
- Advertise your services. If you like to type or edit papers or tutor other students, why not get paid for it? Put up posters around campus that show students what you are offering and how much you charge.

Post on university social media accounts and local online resources.

No matter what route you take to make more money, try to find one that doesn't interfere too much with your schoolwork. If you are having trouble finding the time to go to class or to do your homework, try cutting back on your hours at work.

Another component of reducing stress and maximizing your time is effectively managing your money. Whether it comes from mom and dad or your hard-earned paycheck, money management for college students is essential to learn.

Money Tips

Money certainly makes the world go round, and we all need to be mindful of how much money we have and where all of it is going. Money management is especially necessary for college students. College expenses are ridiculously high with tuition, books, fees, parking, room and board, rent, gas, date money, movie rentals, etc. Effective money management is made easier with these tips.

First, track your spending for two to four weeks to find out where your money is going. Ask yourself if seven or eight trips to Starbucks a week is really necessary? You probably don't realize how much money you spend on little things like snacks and drinks. Often, just by tracking expenses, you'll start to curb your expenses and spend your money more effectively.

· · ·

THE BEST WAY TO manage your money for a semester is to sit down and map out a budget. List sources of income such as scholarships, loans, money from summer jobs, and cash from your parents. Then list your expenses, such as tuition, books, and groceries. If your income is larger than your spending, you're on the right track!

GOING TO BUY NEW CLOTHES, going to a concert, or movie... make room for that in your budget. After all, you do need some fun and entertainment in your life. You'll get burned out if you don't have any fun. But be mindful of your entertainment expenses so that they don't get out of hand.

IF YOU SPEND, spend, spend at the beginning of the semester, you will be broke later in the term. Give yourself a spending limit for each week. Stick to it, and you won't have to eat macaroni-and-cheese every day in December.

BE careful with credit card use. Having a credit card is a good idea in case of emergencies, but having that little piece of plastic can make your spending get way out of control, very, very quick. One quick way to spend beyond your means is to charge it. Use credit cards sparingly. Once you get into the habit of reaching for plastic, it can be hard to stop.

KEEP ONLY ONE CREDIT CARD. You'll receive countless offers from credit card companies wanting to give you credit at recklessly high-interest rates to celebrate your arrival into the "real world." Find a card with a low-interest rate and use it as little as possible. And don't charge small purchases! You don't want to be paying interest on a cup of coffee!

IF YOU'RE AFRAID, you'll keep spending as long as there's room on the card, call your credit card company and request your credit limit be lowered. Keep at it. Card companies will try to boost up your credit lines, so you spend more. Just say "no" each time they try.

BE realistic about your spending habits. You can do what you want, but you can't do everything you want. You're going to have to make some choices. Whatever you choose it is going to cost some money. You need to understand you can't have everything and you have to understand there are consequences.

MAKE up for it next week if you blow your budget on something you want to do this week. If you go out to dinner and a movie one week, spend the money, be happy with your decision, then commit to staying at home the next week, eating at home, and not making any extra expenditures.

MAKE A BUDGET FOR LARGE PURCHASES. If you know a significant purchase is coming up, whether it's a road trip with friends or a car insurance premium, start putting money aside to cover it. It's far easier to save $50 each month than to come up with $600 when the payment is due.

BEFORE THE SEMESTER BEGINS, talk to your roommate about dorm or apartment expenses and divide them up. Decide who is bringing a refrigerator and who is bringing a microwave, and so on. This way, you may avoid making duplicate purchases and overspending while still having all the comforts that make college life easy.

THE MAJORITY of the large expenses occur at the start of the school year. Remember to compare pricing at online bookstores. They might be able to offer you a better rate than the bookstore on campus. Whenever possible, buy used books. Use the ISBN of the textbooks you need to search Amazon, Ebay, or Half.com. This number may usually be obtained through your college bookstore, and the prices are usually significantly lower than those charged by the bookstore.

REMEMBER that if you have a book you don't believe you'll use again once the semester is done - Thermonuclear Dynamics, The History of the Hobbit, etc. – you can sell it back to the school or advertise it online. Selling your books at the end of the semester can be a simple way to make some extra cash.

IT IS preferable to get assistance sooner rather than later. "I'm in difficulties and need $2,000," or "I spent my student loan money on an amazing spring break trip" are difficult to convey. The longer you wait, the worse it will become. While your parents may be upset that you've been so irresponsible with your money, I'm willing to bet that they'll be happy to assist you — after a lecture and tongue lashing, of course!

KEEP in mind that managing money is essentially about managing resources. Also, keep in mind that money normally functions on at least two levels within us. There's the practical side of things, where we buy things. There's also the metaphorical level to consider. Money may provide us with pleasure, friendships, and a sense of power. We must be careful not to let money take the place of emotional demands that must be met in other ways.

IF MONEY IS TIGHT, you can do several simple things every day to save money and avoid a financial crisis.

- Avoid eating fast food every day. Take a look at the school's cafeteria's meal plans. Purchase items that are quick and easy to prepare in your room.
- Clip coupons for items you buy frequently and keep them in your car so you may use them at the supermarket, fast food, or restaurants.
- Rather than going to the movies, watch a movie online.
- Consolidate errands to save money on gasoline. When you do need to get petrol, go to a station with a lot of competition nearby to enhance your chances of receiving the best deal.
- Stock up on items you know you'll need later at holiday and back-to-school bargains.
- If you can save money by switching carriers or getting a new cell phone plan, do so.
- When shopping, use a shopping list and stick to it as much as possible. • Keep an eye on the register when checking out at stores; purchases can easily scan wrongly.

FINALLY, as absurd as it may sound, considering college is a time of financial constraints, consider putting a little money aside weekly. A hundred and four dollars is still two dollars a week at the end of the year. Then, either for yourself or with someone else, do something exceptionally pleasant.

SAVING IS ALSO a form of spending. Check out these quick money-management ideas to see if they can't help you attain your college goals and ambitions. It is frequently stated, "You can manage your life by managing your time. You ruin your life by wasting your time." "Manage it, don't let it manage you," we should say when it comes to money. Now let's get down to business — having fun, making time for fun, and making the most of your college experience!

Party Responsibly

Parties and socializing are a big part of student life. And contrary to some people's thoughts, you should not deny yourself the right to enjoy the non-academic side of the university. However, some students are placed on probation or kicked out of school every semester due to poor decisions and actions taken while under the influence.   It would be best to keep in mind that partying is only a small part of the college experience. It has its pitfalls, and you need to be careful not to overdo it to affect your goals and future negatively.

WHEN YOU HAVE AN EARLY CLASS, avoid the bars the night before. You're just setting yourself up for trouble if you don't. Even if you do get up the next morning after a late night out, you won't be able to focus on your classes. The lack of focus will result in missing important information that you will need later on. Also, you won't be performing to your full potential if you're tired or hungover.

BE mindful of the downfalls of excessive alcohol use. I am not saying you have to avoid alcohol completely. If you're of legal age and you want to enjoy a drink or two, by all means, go ahead. But, it's easy for a few drinks to turn into a few more, and before you know it, you've developed a problem.

WARNING signs that alcohol may be a problem include:

- Missing classes or appointments
- Declining grades
- Aggressive behavior while drunk
- Erratic behavior while drinking
- Blacking out or poor recollection of events
- Drinking when under stress

IF YOU THINK you might have a problem, don't hesitate to seek help. Most college campuses have counselors on staff to help with problems affecting college students. Talk to your family doctor or attend an Alcoholics Anonymous meeting.

NEVER, ever drink and drive. Take an Uber, Lyft, or cab, take turns with your friends being designated driver, or walk (but be careful – you CAN get a ticket for public intoxication if you're too smashed!) Safety should be first and foremost in your mind – at all costs! Bad things do happen both on and off-campus. Always be safe and stay with a group.

. . .

THERE'S MUCH MORE to college life than partying, though. Enjoy the other aspects of the university. Join an organization that seems interesting and where you will find like-minded students. Were you student body president in high school? Look into the student council or get involved in campus politics. If you're interested in acting, consider student theater productions interested in business, technology, marketing, there is a club for that. Most colleges have hundreds of clubs ranging from soccer to science, spend some time on your universities website and check out clubs on display during orientation and other times of the year on campus.

SORORITIES AND FRATERNITIES are present on most four-year campuses. These are great places to make new friendships that can last for a lifetime. There's often a "rush" week during which time you can visit the houses and learn more about which groups you might want to join.

OFTEN, there is a voting process during which you will be accepted or rejected. Don't be discouraged if things don't work out on your first try. It is not a personal statement on your worth. Just don't give up. Being part of a fraternity or sorority can be great fun and a huge learning experience.

DON'T DISCOUNT LAID-BACK activities as well. Simply watching a movie or playing video games with your dorm-mates can be great relaxation and just as fun as going to a bar – but without the hangover!

. . .

HAVING fun is a big part of college life. You deserve to enjoy the whole experience, so be sure to make time for yourself and develop friendships and new interests.

So, what if you're a non-traditional student? Think this advice doesn't apply to you? Let's address that in our next section.

Tips for Non-traditional Students

Many older adults are going back to college to complete degrees they started years ago, fulfill a lifelong ambition, or train for a new career path. Time management for non-traditional students is especially crucial as the issue of children and family contributes to the already hectic life of a full-time college student. Some non-traditional students also juggle full-time jobs along with their studies. Finding time to study, take care of a home, work an outside job, and have a personal life seems out of reach. However, time management skills make it not only possible but also realistic.

REFER to the section in this book regarding using your planner. Having a planner and referring to it often is more crucial than ever with other activities going on in your lives. You will also want to invest in a dry erase board for your home in a calendar format to keep track of events, appointments, and homework assignments. Calendaring can be especially helpful so that your family always knows where you are. Keep the board in a convenient, well-referred place such as the refrigerator or by the front door.

.   .   .

USE a different color marker for each family member so you know who is where and when. List your class schedule on the dry erase board and have your family members record their activities along with times to keep track of everyone's schedule. It's a good idea to copy this same schedule down in your planner since your planner should always be with you, and you will always know how to schedule your hectic life.

REMEMBER why you are in college in the first place and make this a priority in your life. It would help if you talked with family and friends to understand that even though they matter tremendously to you, your schoolwork is a priority, and their support is needed.

ALLOT a specific time each day for studying. You need a quiet place with minimal distractions. You may want to physically write your study schedule on the dry erase board as well. Let your family know that when you're studying, you must be left alone. Then do nothing else during that time. Shut off the phone, stay put, and concentrate on your studies.

ORGANIZATION SKILLS ARE another key component to effective time management. While we have a whole section in this book on organization, some special attention needs to be taken to address your circumstances. You need to identify one specific place to keep all your books and reference materials. Keep a separate bag or backpack to hold that day's books and anything you need for class.

. . .

WHEN YOU STUDY, designate a separate study space where you can be away from your family. The key is to eliminate all distractions and focus on your schoolwork. Make sure you keep a supply of paper and pencils nearby this space as well.

TAKE ADVANTAGE OF "DOWN" time. You can study on your lunch break at work, while watching your child's soccer game, sitting in the doctor's office, or anywhere you have waiting time. Of course, in your car, commuting to class is probably a bad idea!

YOU MIGHT BE apprehensive and even nervous about returning to school, but realize that this is a normal reaction. You're returning to a setting you haven't seen in a while, and when you get there, you'll be with much younger people, which can seem overwhelming. Don't feel alone. Look around the campus. I'd bet you're not the only one there.

CHANCES ARE, the traditional college student won't care that you're older than they are. Once the class is in full swing, and you are part of the class environment, you may be surprised when some younger students come to you for help and advice.

TAKE advantage of all the resources your college has to offer, such as computer labs, library resources, help centers, and tutors. Don't be afraid to ask for help – especially from your professors. If you do not understand something in the class, arrange a meeting when your professor has office hours. Most instructors are more than willing to help out their students – especially the non-traditional ones!

· · ·

ALMOST EVERY COLLEGE has a program for the non-traditional student that helps with adjusting to college life, honing your study skills, and dealing with the pressures of juggling studies, family, and work. Use these services as they are designed to help YOU!

8

TIME MANAGEMENT TOOLS

T echnology has blessed us with many opportunities to enhance our time management skills. There are many tools available to us on the Internet that we can use every day to save time and make the most of our day. Let's look at twelve of the most important apps and tools you can use to help your time management.

Google Drive

Google Drive is a tool that backs up all your files. It comes with 15 GB of free space that can store anything that you have in the cloud. It is an excellent organizational tool that allows you to file many different items and put them in the right place. You can also create documents, Excel spreadsheets, and PowerPoint presentations. These items can be downloaded and saved to your computer or USB and sent to people via email. If you want to consolidate all of your items, you can do it using Google Drive. Then, you will be able to access the files anywhere you go. It is practical, efficient, and safe to use.

Evernote

Evernote is an effective tool for storing notes from lectures and to-do lists, among other things. All the items are effectively stored in the cloud, which allows you easy access. You can also organize your notes, so you don't have to sort through every file one by one. Also, you can pull it up on your mobile device or computer (O'Donovan, 2020).

MindNode

Have you ever heard of mind-mapping? This tool helps you map out your day, activities, and goals. It allows you to put everything in one place to do your work efficiently.

My Life Organized (MLO)

Looking for a way to sort through your ever-increasing to-do list? Look no further than the app, My Life Organized, which will help you effectively create to-do lists that are all consolidated in one place, so you won't be aimlessly going through life (O'Donovan, 2020).

1Password

Do you find yourself frequently forgetting your password to different apps and websites? Forget no more with this app, which uses one password to store all your passwords in one secure place, so you'll never forget your passwords again. You can easily pull up the app with your 1Password app, and then you'll save time and memory.

Pocket – Keep Your Eye on the Ball

Have you ever found a website that you liked and wanted to save for future reference? Pocket consolidates the websites you want to view and makes it easier for you to access later. Then, you won't lose the websites you just looked at and have to search for them again (O'Donovan, 2020).

Focus@Will

This app boosts your attention span and enables you to focus on the tasks at hand through interactive activities that will greatly benefit your life.

Alfred

With this tool, you can intelligently interact with your computer because you use small keystrokes and commands to access your documents, perform scans, and other computer activities. It is an effective way to save time and energy. Plus, you have the feel-good experience of knowing you are "high-tech."

TimeTree

This interactive tool lets you share calendars, to-do lists, and other key information with family members. There is no more needing to give a paper to someone. Instead, you can use your phone or computer and share everything with your friends and family. It is highly effective.

Todoist

Todoist is a great tool to capture and order all your activities to be consolidated into one big to-do list that will keep you organized. This tool works wonders for you, as you need to write down your to-do list on a piece of paper or in your notepad (O'Donovan, 2020).

Trello

Trello is an app that helps you chart your progress on various projects and tasks on your to-do list. You can create cards that represent what you need to do and then watch as you put status symbols like To Do, In Progress, or Completed. It's a motivating way to stay organized.

Forest

In this app, you will build a digital forest, representing the tasks on your to-do list and your success in completing them. You plant a digital tree and watch it grow. If you stay focused and complete your assignments, then the tree will grow. If you lose your focus, the tree will too. Using this digital tool, you will feel that you are creating something that needs nutrition and sustenance. It is a great metaphor for your life (O'Donovan, 2020).

TECHNOLOGY TOOLS ARE useful in our everyday lives. They make simple tasks much easier to accomplish. We might find ourselves unable to manage our time well, but it is possible to make a meaningful life and do tasks much more efficiently and quickly with the preceding twelve tools. Because of today's fast-paced world, time is of the essence, and we must find ways to cut down on useless time spent doing tasks that bear no meaning or significance. Therefore, it is crucial to find ways to save time that will benefit us in the long run. Use technology to save you a lot of time and trouble, so you have more time for yourself to enjoy life.

CONCLUSION

Thank you for purchasing this book!

I hope you have enjoyed reading it and that it has been helpful and valuable in teaching you how to be more efficient with your time.

The next step is to continue practicing what you have learned, and in doing so, you will continue to increase your productivity and live a happier life.

Finally, if you enjoyed this book, giving a review online would be greatly appreciated!

Thank you and good luck!

CPSIA information can be obtained
at www.ICGtesting.com
Printed in the USA
BVHW031110260722
643032BV00015B/799

9 781088 023488